ELIJAH L. COOLEY

CYBERSECURITY, HACKING, AND DIGITAL DEFENSE

A Complete Guide to Cybersecurity, Ethical Hacking, and Advanced Cyber Defense Strategies

This book is dedicated to the warriors of the digital age—the ethical hackers, cybersecurity professionals, and defenders of the internet who work tirelessly to protect the world from unseen threats. To those who stand on the front lines of cyber warfare, digital forensics, and network defense, your efforts ensure the safety and integrity of our digital future.

Contents

Foreword

The **digital battlefield is constantly evolving**. Every day, **governments, corporations, and individuals face an increasing wave of cyber threats**, ranging from **data breaches and ransomware attacks to nation-state cyber warfare and AI-powered hacking campaigns**. The world is more connected than ever before, and with that connectivity comes **an ever-expanding attack surface** that demands **a new generation of cybersecurity professionals** capable of **defending, innovating, and staying ahead of cyber adversaries**.

This book was born from **a mission to bridge the gap between cybersecurity theory and real-world application**. It is not just a **technical guide**—it is a **mastery roadmap**, designed for those who seek **not only knowledge but the ability to act, defend, and innovate in the field of cybersecurity**. Whether you are a **beginner learning foundational concepts, an ethical hacker refining your penetration testing skills, or a cybersecurity leader preparing for the next wave of digital threats**, this book will equip you with **the strategies, methodologies, and tools needed to excel in cybersecurity**.

As cybercriminals evolve, so must we. The **future of cybersecurity belongs to those who dare to push boundaries, challenge security norms, and commit to continuous learning**. This book is your **weapon in the fight against cyber threats, your guide to building a resilient career, and your key to unlocking cybersecurity mastery**.

Prepare to **learn, apply, and lead**. The digital battlefield awaits.

— **Elijah L. Cooley**

Chapter 1

INTRODUCTION TO CYBERSECURITY

1.1 What is Cybersecurity?

Cybersecurity is the practice of **protecting systems, networks, and digital assets from cyber threats, unauthorized access, data breaches, and malicious attacks**. It encompasses a broad range of disciplines, including **network security, application security, cryptography, ethical hacking, and digital forensics**.

Cyber threats have evolved significantly, affecting governments, corporations, and individuals alike. Cybercriminals, nation-state actors, and hacktivists continuously develop **new attack techniques** that exploit system vulnerabilities. As a result, cybersecurity has become a **global priority**, with industries investing in **cyber defense strategies, threat intelligence, and advanced security technologies** to mitigate risks.

Key Objectives of Cybersecurity

1. **Confidentiality:** Ensuring that sensitive information is only accessible to authorized users.
2. **Integrity:** Protecting data from unauthorized modification or corruption.
3. **Availability:** Ensuring that critical systems and data remain accessible

to authorized users.

4. **Authentication:** Verifying user identities to prevent unauthorized access.

5. **Non-Repudiation:** Ensuring that actions taken within a system can be attributed to a specific user or entity.

Cybersecurity professionals work to **identify, mitigate, and prevent cyber risks**, safeguarding digital assets from attacks that could lead to financial loss, reputational damage, and legal consequences.

1.2 The Growing Importance of Cybersecurity

The world has become increasingly dependent on **digital technologies**, making cybersecurity more critical than ever. The rise of **cloud computing, artificial intelligence, blockchain, and the Internet of Things (IoT)** has introduced new vulnerabilities that hackers exploit to compromise systems.

Factors Driving the Need for Cybersecurity

1. **Increased Cybercrime:** Ransomware, phishing, and data breaches have become more frequent, causing billions of dollars in damages annually.

2. **State-Sponsored Cyber Warfare:** Nation-states engage in cyber espionage, infrastructure attacks, and disinformation campaigns.

3. **Data Privacy Regulations:** Laws such as **GDPR, CCPA, and HIPAA** require organizations to implement stringent security measures to protect user data.

4. **Cloud and IoT Vulnerabilities:** The expansion of **cloud-based services** and **smart devices** has introduced new security risks.

5. **Financial and Economic Impact:** Cyber attacks disrupt businesses, affect stock markets, and lead to **major economic losses**.

The **cybersecurity industry** is expected to grow exponentially, with an increasing demand for professionals skilled in **ethical hacking, penetration**

testing, and cyber defense. Governments and corporations invest heavily in **cybersecurity research and development** to stay ahead of evolving threats.

1.3 Common Cybersecurity Myths and Misconceptions

Despite its importance, cybersecurity remains **widely misunderstood**. Many individuals and businesses still believe in **dangerous myths** that leave them vulnerable to attacks.

Myth #1: "I am not a target because I am not famous or wealthy."

Reality: Cybercriminals do not only target high-profile individuals or large corporations. **Hackers use automated tools to scan the internet for vulnerable systems**, making **anyone** a potential target. Personal data, bank accounts, and even **social media accounts** are valuable assets to cybercriminals.

Myth #2: "Antivirus software alone will protect me."

Reality: While antivirus software is essential, it does not provide **complete protection**. Attackers use **zero-day exploits, phishing attacks, and social engineering tactics** that bypass traditional antivirus defenses. A **multi-layered security approach** is required for effective protection.

Myth #3: "Strong passwords are enough to secure my accounts."

Reality: While strong passwords help, **password-based authentication alone is not secure**. Cybercriminals use **brute-force attacks, credential stuffing, and password leaks** to compromise accounts. Implementing **multi-factor authentication (MFA)** significantly enhances security.

Myth #4: "Only hackers need to understand cybersecurity."

Reality: Cybersecurity knowledge is critical for **everyone**, not just hackers and IT professionals. **Businesses, employees, and individuals** must understand **cyber hygiene, secure practices, and digital risk management** to prevent attacks.

Myth #5: "Cybersecurity is only about technology."

Reality: While technology plays a major role, cybersecurity also involves **human behavior, legal policies, risk management, and governance**. Many cyber attacks exploit **human psychology** rather than technical weaknesses. **Security awareness training** is as important as technological defenses.

1.4 Careers in Cybersecurity and Ethical Hacking

The cybersecurity field offers **diverse career opportunities**, ranging from **defensive security roles** to **offensive security experts**. Organizations actively recruit cybersecurity professionals due to the increasing number of cyber threats.

Career Paths in Cybersecurity

1. **Penetration Tester (Ethical Hacker):** Simulates cyber attacks to identify vulnerabilities in systems.
2. **Security Analyst:** Monitors and protects networks from cyber threats.
3. **Incident Responder:** Investigates and mitigates cyber attacks in real time.
4. **Cryptographer:** Develops encryption algorithms and secure communication protocols.
5. **Security Engineer:** Designs and implements security architectures for organizations.
6. **Forensic Analyst:** Investigates cybercrimes and gathers digital evidence.

7. **Threat Intelligence Analyst:** Tracks hacker activities and underground cybercrime networks.

Cybersecurity professionals must **continuously learn and adapt** to new threats. Certifications such as **Certified Ethical Hacker (CEH), Offensive Security Certified Professional (OSCP), and Certified Information Systems Security Professional (CISSP)** help professionals advance in the field.

Conclusion

Cybersecurity is an **ever-evolving field** that plays a crucial role in protecting individuals, businesses, and nations from cyber threats. As attackers develop **more sophisticated methods**, cybersecurity professionals must continuously enhance their skills and adopt **proactive security strategies**.

In the next chapter, we will **explore different types of cyber threats, hacking techniques, and how attackers exploit vulnerabilities**. Understanding the **tactics, tools, and procedures (TTPs)** used by cybercriminals is the first step in building a **strong cyber defense strategy**.

Proceed to Chapter 2: Understanding Cyber Threats and Attack Vectors for an in-depth analysis of **malware, ransomware, phishing, advanced persistent threats (APTs), and real-world hacking techniques**.

Chapter 2

UNDERSTANDING CYBER THREATS AND ATTACK VECTORS

2.1 The Evolution of Cyber Threats

Cyber threats have evolved significantly over the past few decades, progressing from simple viruses and worms to highly sophisticated **nation-state cyberattacks, ransomware-as-a-service (RaaS), and artificial intelligence-powered malware**. The rise of cloud computing, mobile technology, and interconnected devices has increased the attack surface, allowing cybercriminals to exploit new vulnerabilities.

Hackers have developed **coordinated attack techniques**, combining **social engineering, zero-day vulnerabilities, supply chain exploits, and artificial intelligence** to breach even the most secure networks. Organizations must **constantly adapt their cybersecurity strategies** to counteract these evolving threats.

2.2 Types of Cyber Threats

Cyber threats can be classified into several categories based on their impact, attack methods, and intent. Understanding these threats is essential for implementing effective cybersecurity measures.

2.2.1 Malware (Malicious Software)

Malware is a broad term used to describe **any software designed to cause harm** to a computer, network, or digital system. Malware includes viruses, worms, ransomware, trojans, spyware, and rootkits.

Viruses

A **virus** is a type of malware that **attaches itself to legitimate files or programs and spreads when the infected file is executed**. Once activated, it can corrupt, delete, or steal data.

Example of how a virus spreads:

1. A user unknowingly downloads an infected file from an email attachment.
2. The virus executes upon opening the file and starts modifying system files.
3. The virus replicates and spreads to other connected systems via network shares or USB devices.

Worms

A **worm** is a self-replicating program that spreads across networks without requiring user interaction. Unlike viruses, worms **do not need to attach themselves to existing files**.

Example of a worm attack:

- The **WannaCry ransomware worm** exploited the **EternalBlue vulnerability** in Windows systems, spreading rapidly across the internet in 2017.

Trojans

A **trojan** is malware that **disguises itself as legitimate software** but contains hidden malicious functionality. Trojans often create **backdoors** that allow attackers to gain remote access to a compromised system.

Common types of trojans:

- **Remote Access Trojans (RATs):** Allow attackers to take full control of an infected system.
- **Banking Trojans:** Steal financial credentials from users.
- **Spyware:** Monitors user activity and collects sensitive information.

Ransomware

Ransomware is one of the most **destructive forms of malware**, encrypting a victim's files and demanding a ransom payment in cryptocurrency. **Sophisticated ransomware operations**, such as **REvil, DarkSide, and Conti,** have targeted hospitals, banks, and government agencies.

Stages of a ransomware attack:

1. **Initial infection:** Delivered via phishing emails, malicious links, or drive-by downloads.
2. **Encryption process:** The malware encrypts files using strong cryptographic algorithms.
3. **Ransom demand:** Attackers display a ransom note demanding payment for decryption keys.
4. **Double extortion:** Some ransomware groups **steal data before encryption**, threatening to leak it if the ransom is not paid.

Real-world example:

- The **Colonial Pipeline attack (2021)** disrupted fuel supply in the United States, leading to widespread panic and financial loss.

2.2.2 Phishing and Social Engineering Attacks

Phishing is a cyber attack that tricks individuals into **revealing sensitive information** by impersonating trusted entities. Phishing attacks are highly effective because they exploit human psychology rather than technical vulnerabilities.

Common Types of Phishing Attacks:

- **Email Phishing:** Attackers send emails posing as legitimate companies (e.g., banks, government agencies) to steal credentials.
- **Spear Phishing:** A targeted attack designed to trick specific individuals within an organization.
- **Whaling:** A phishing attack aimed at high-level executives, such as CEOs or CFOs.
- **Smishing:** Phishing via SMS messages, often containing malicious links.
- **Vishing:** Voice-based phishing where attackers impersonate trusted individuals over the phone.

Example of an Email Phishing Attack:

1. A user receives an email claiming to be from their bank, asking them to **verify their account** due to suspicious activity.
2. The email contains a **fake login page** that mimics the bank's official website.
3. When the user enters their credentials, the attacker captures the information and gains access to the account.

How to Defend Against Phishing:

- Verify the sender's email address before clicking any links.
- Use **multi-factor authentication (MFA)** to protect accounts.
- Train employees on how to recognize phishing attempts.

2.2.3 Denial-of-Service (DoS) and Distributed Denial-of-Service (DDoS) Attacks

A **Denial-of-Service (DoS) attack** aims to overwhelm a system, server, or network by flooding it with excessive traffic, rendering it **unusable**.

A **Distributed Denial-of-Service (DDoS) attack** is a more powerful version of a DoS attack, where **multiple compromised devices (botnets) coordinate to attack a target simultaneously**.

Real-world example:

- The **Mirai Botnet (2016)** used **IoT devices** to launch massive **DDoS attacks**, taking down major websites such as Twitter, Netflix, and PayPal.

Mitigating DoS and DDoS Attacks:

- Use **firewalls and intrusion prevention systems (IPS)** to filter malicious traffic.
- Deploy **DDoS protection services** such as Cloudflare or AWS Shield.
- Rate-limit incoming traffic to prevent server overload.

2.2.4 Advanced Persistent Threats (APTs)

APTs are sophisticated, long-term cyber attacks conducted by nation-state actors or highly skilled cybercriminal groups. These attackers infiltrate networks **undetected** and remain inside for extended periods, collecting intelligence, stealing data, or sabotaging operations.

Characteristics of APTs:

- **Targeted attacks:** Focused on government agencies, defense contractors, and multinational corporations.
- **Multi-phase operations:** Use **social engineering, malware, and zero-day exploits** to gain access.
- **Persistence:** Attackers establish **backdoors and stealth mechanisms** to

avoid detection.

Real-World APT Examples:

- **APT29 (Cozy Bear)** – Linked to Russian intelligence agencies, involved in the **SolarWinds supply chain attack (2020)**.
- **APT41 (Chinese cyber espionage group)** – Targeted financial, healthcare, and gaming industries.

Defending Against APTs:

- Implement **network segmentation** to limit access to critical systems.
- Conduct **continuous monitoring and threat intelligence analysis**.
- Deploy **endpoint detection and response (EDR) solutions** to identify suspicious activity.

2.3 The Future of Cyber Threats

Cyber threats will continue to evolve, driven by **artificial intelligence, quantum computing, and automation**.

Emerging Threats:

1. **AI-Generated Cyber Attacks:** Hackers will use **machine learning algorithms** to develop adaptive malware.
2. **Deepfake Social Engineering:** Attackers will create **convincing deepfake videos and audio** for fraud and misinformation.
3. **Quantum Computing Threats: Quantum decryption algorithms** could break traditional cryptographic systems.

Organizations must **invest in proactive cybersecurity strategies** to stay ahead of evolving threats.

Conclusion

Understanding cyber threats is the **first step in developing effective cybersecurity defenses**. Attackers constantly refine their tactics, making it critical for individuals and organizations to **stay informed, implement best security practices, and adopt advanced cybersecurity solutions**.

In **Chapter 3: Fundamentals of Ethical Hacking**, we will explore how ethical hackers use penetration testing methodologies to identify vulnerabilities before cybercriminals exploit them. Proceed to the next chapter for an in-depth study of **ethical hacking principles, attack simulations, and security assessment techniques**.

Chapter 3

FUNDAMENTALS OF ETHICAL HACKING

3.1 Introduction to Ethical Hacking

Ethical hacking is the **legally authorized practice of testing, analyzing, and securing digital systems, networks, and applications by simulating real-world cyber attacks**. Ethical hackers identify vulnerabilities before malicious attackers can exploit them, ensuring security defenses remain strong.

Organizations hire **ethical hackers, also known as penetration testers or white-hat hackers**, to conduct controlled security assessments and **mitigate risks**. Ethical hacking requires **technical expertise, problem-solving skills, and deep knowledge of cyber threats, vulnerabilities, and exploitation techniques**.

Ethical Hacking vs. Malicious Hacking

Ethical hacking differs from black-hat hacking in its intent and authorization.

Ethical Hacking	Malicious Hacking
Legally authorized and performed with consent.	Conducted without permission, violating laws.
Aims to improve cybersecurity defenses.	Aims to steal, destroy, or exploit data.
Adheres to ethical and legal standards.	Operates outside of legal boundaries.
Conducted by security professionals with certifications.	Conducted by cybercriminals or unauthorized actors.

Why Ethical Hacking is Critical

Prevents **data breaches and financial loss**.

Strengthens an organization's **security posture**.

Helps **comply with cybersecurity regulations** such as **PCI-DSS, HIPAA, and GDPR**.

Simulates **real-world attack scenarios** to test **defensive capabilities**.

Ethical hacking plays a **key role in modern cybersecurity** by ensuring that organizations remain **one step ahead of cybercriminals**.

3.2 The Five Phases of Ethical Hacking

Ethical hacking follows a structured process, ensuring **thorough security assessments** without disrupting operations. These five phases align with **penetration testing methodologies** used by security professionals worldwide.

Phase 1: Reconnaissance (Information Gathering)

Reconnaissance is the process of **gathering intelligence about a target system, organization, or individual** before launching an attack. Ethical hackers use **open-source intelligence (OSINT), footprinting, and passive scanning** to identify **potential entry points**.

Types of Reconnaissance:

Passive Reconnaissance: Collecting data without interacting directly with the target.

Searching public records, WHOIS databases, and social media.

Monitoring network traffic through third-party tools.

Active Reconnaissance: Interacting with the target system to gather detailed information.

Scanning networks with **Nmap** and **Shodan** to detect open ports.

Conducting email harvesting using tools like **theHarvester**.

Real-World Example:

In **2013, hackers used passive reconnaissance to gather employee credentials** from social media before launching phishing attacks against major corporations.

Phase 2: Scanning and Enumeration

Once reconnaissance is complete, ethical hackers scan and enumerate targets to **identify live systems, vulnerabilities, and exploitable services**.

Common Scanning Techniques:

Network Scanning: Identifying active hosts, open ports, and network topology using **Nmap, Angry IP Scanner, and Masscan**.

Vulnerability Scanning: Detecting software flaws with **Nessus, OpenVAS, and Qualys**.

- **Banner Grabbing:** Retrieving system details from **HTTP, FTP, and SMTP servers** to determine software versions.

Example of Network Scanning:

1. An ethical hacker uses **Nmap** to scan a company's external IP range:

```
CSS

nmap -sV -A -T4 <target-ip>
```

The scan reveals **open SSH, FTP, and MySQL ports**, indicating possible misconfigurations.

Phase 3: Gaining Access (Exploitation)

During this phase, ethical hackers **attempt to exploit vulnerabilities** to gain unauthorized access to the system. **Penetration testing frameworks like Metasploit, SQLMap, and Hydra** are commonly used.

Types of Exploits Used in Penetration Testing:

Operating System Exploits: Exploiting unpatched software vulnerabilities.

Web Application Exploits: Attacking **SQL injection (SQLi), cross-site scripting (XSS), and insecure authentication mechanisms**.

Brute-Force Attacks: Guessing credentials using **Hydra, John the Ripper, and Hashcat**.

Real-World Example:

The **Equifax Data Breach (2017)** occurred because attackers exploited an **Apache Struts vulnerability** that had not been patched, leading to the exposure of **147 million customer records**.

Phase 4: Maintaining Access (Persistence)

Once access is gained, hackers may establish **backdoors or privilege escalation techniques** to maintain long-term access. Ethical hackers test for persistence to **identify real-world threats** before cybercriminals can exploit them.

Common Persistence Techniques:

Creating new user accounts with administrative privileges.

Embedding malware into legitimate applications.

Deploying remote access trojans (RATs) for continuous control.

Ethical hackers document these findings and **recommend mitigation strategies** to prevent real-world exploitation.

Phase 5: Covering Tracks and Reporting

In real-world cyber attacks, malicious hackers erase logs and traces to avoid detection. Ethical hackers simulate these techniques but **document findings instead of causing harm**.

Key Aspects of Covering Tracks:

Clearing system logs using PowerShell or Linux commands.

Disabling security alerts and forensic tools.

Encrypting communication to avoid detection.

Once testing is complete, ethical hackers generate **a detailed penetration**

testing report outlining:

Discovered vulnerabilities and exploits.

Technical severity ratings and business impact analysis.

Recommendations for remediation and security best practices.

3.3 Tools and Technologies Used in Ethical Hacking

Ethical hackers use a variety of **penetration testing tools** to automate reconnaissance, scanning, exploitation, and reporting.

Essential Ethical Hacking Tools:

Category	Tool Name	Purpose
Reconnaissance	Shodan	Identifies internet-exposed assets.
Network Scanning	Nmap	Scans open ports and services.
Web Exploitation	Burp Suite	Identifies web application vulnerabilities.
Exploitation	Metasploit	Automates penetration testing attacks.
Password Cracking	Hashcat	Cracks hashed passwords efficiently.
Post-Exploitation	Empire	Establishes persistence on compromised systems.

Each tool plays a **critical role in penetration testing**, allowing ethical hackers to identify security flaws **before they are exploited by attackers**.

3.4 Ethical Hacking Certifications and Career Pathways

Becoming an ethical hacker requires **technical expertise, hands-on experience, and industry-recognized certifications**.

Top Ethical Hacking Certifications:

- **Certified Ethical Hacker (CEH):** Covers penetration testing methodologies and security principles.
- **Offensive Security Certified Professional (OSCP):** Focuses on hands-on

penetration testing with real-world challenges.
- **GIAC Penetration Tester (GPEN):** Validates advanced ethical hacking skills.

Career Roles in Ethical Hacking:

- **Penetration Tester:** Conducts simulated cyber attacks.
- **Red Team Operator:** Emulates adversary tactics to test security defenses.
- **Security Consultant:** Advises businesses on cybersecurity strategies.

Ethical hacking offers **lucrative career opportunities**, with organizations increasingly investing in cybersecurity professionals to defend against **growing cyber threats**.

Conclusion

Ethical hacking is a **critical component of cybersecurity**, enabling organizations to identify vulnerabilities before cybercriminals exploit them. By following **penetration testing methodologies, using advanced tools, and obtaining ethical hacking certifications**, cybersecurity professionals can **protect digital systems from evolving threats**.

In **Chapter 4: Penetration Testing Methodologies**, we will explore **real-world penetration testing frameworks, red teaming strategies, and advanced exploitation techniques** used by ethical hackers and cybersecurity professionals worldwide.

Chapter 4

PENETRATION TESTING METHODOLOGIES

4.1 Introduction to Penetration Testing

Penetration testing, also known as **pen testing or ethical hacking**, is a **systematic process of simulating cyber attacks on an organization's infrastructure, applications, and networks to identify vulnerabilities before real attackers exploit them**. Unlike conventional security assessments, penetration testing involves actively attempting to **bypass security controls, escalate privileges, and exfiltrate sensitive data** under controlled conditions.

Penetration tests provide organizations with:

- **A realistic evaluation of security defenses.**
- **A clear understanding of exploitable weaknesses.**
- **Actionable recommendations to mitigate risks before a breach occurs.**

Penetration testing is **not random hacking** but follows **structured methodologies, ethical guidelines, and legal parameters** to ensure thorough security assessments without disrupting business operations.

4.2 Types of Penetration Testing

Penetration testing varies based on **scope, target environment, and testing objectives**. Ethical hackers conduct **different types of penetration tests** depending on the specific security concerns of an organization.

4.2.1 Network Penetration Testing

Network penetration testing focuses on evaluating **external and internal network infrastructures** for vulnerabilities that could be exploited by attackers.
  Objectives:

- Identify **misconfigured firewalls, open ports, and unpatched services**.
- Detect **unauthorized access points and weak authentication mechanisms**.
- Simulate **real-world attack scenarios to test an organization's network security posture**.

Common Tools Used:

- **Nmap:** Network mapping and port scanning.
- **Metasploit:** Exploitation of network vulnerabilities.
- **Wireshark:** Network packet analysis for traffic interception.

Example Attack Scenario:
  An ethical hacker scans an organization's external-facing servers and discovers an **open Remote Desktop Protocol (RDP) port**. By **brute-forcing credentials**, they gain access to the internal network, demonstrating a critical security risk.

4.2.2 Web Application Penetration Testing

Web application penetration testing evaluates **websites, APIs, and cloud-based platforms** for security weaknesses that attackers could exploit.
  Objectives:

- Identify **SQL injection (SQLi), cross-site scripting (XSS), and authentication bypass vulnerabilities**.
- Test for **session management flaws and broken access controls**.
- Assess **input validation and server misconfigurations**.

Common Tools Used:

- **Burp Suite:** Web vulnerability scanning and exploitation.
- **SQLMap:** Automated SQL injection testing.
- **OWASP ZAP:** Open-source web application security scanner.

Example Attack Scenario:
  An ethical hacker tests a **banking website's login form** and discovers that entering admin' OR '1'='1 as a username allows **unauthorized access to customer accounts**, revealing an **SQL injection vulnerability**.

4.2.3 Wireless Network Penetration Testing

Wireless penetration testing focuses on evaluating **Wi-Fi networks, Bluetooth connections, and other wireless communications** for vulnerabilities.
  Objectives:

- Identify **weak encryption protocols** such as WEP or improperly configured WPA2 networks.
- Test for **rogue access points that could intercept user traffic**.
- Exploit **wireless authentication mechanisms** to gain unauthorized access.

Common Tools Used:

- **Aircrack-ng:** Cracking Wi-Fi encryption keys.
- **Wireshark:** Sniffing wireless network traffic.
- **Kismet:** Detecting rogue access points and unauthorized connections.

Example Attack Scenario:

An ethical hacker **conducts a deauthentication attack** on a target Wi-Fi network using **aireplay-ng**, forcing devices to disconnect and reconnect. By capturing the handshake, they crack the **Wi-Fi password**, demonstrating poor security configurations.

4.2.4 Social Engineering Penetration Testing

Social engineering penetration testing assesses **human vulnerabilities** by attempting to manipulate employees into **divulging sensitive information, clicking malicious links, or providing unauthorized access**.

Objectives:

- Test an organization's **awareness and training programs**.
- Identify **weak policies that allow attackers to bypass security controls**.
- Simulate **real-world phishing, pretexting, and impersonation attacks**.

Common Techniques Used:

- **Phishing:** Sending emails with malicious links or attachments.
- **Vishing:** Calling employees while impersonating IT support.
- **Physical Social Engineering:** Attempting unauthorized physical entry into secure areas.

Example Attack Scenario:

An ethical hacker **sends a spear-phishing email** to an employee, pretending to be from the IT department. The email contains a **malicious attachment** labeled **"Security Update"**. When opened, the attachment **executes a payload**, granting remote access to the attacker.

4.2.5 Physical Penetration Testing

Physical penetration testing involves attempting to **bypass physical security controls** such as **surveillance systems, RFID badges, and biometric authentication** to access restricted areas.

Objectives:

- Identify **weaknesses in building security policies**.
- Test **physical access control mechanisms**.
- Assess **security awareness among employees and personnel**.

Common Techniques Used:

- **Tailgating:** Entering secure areas by following authorized personnel.
- **Badge Cloning:** Duplicating employee access cards using RFID readers.
- **Lock Picking:** Bypassing physical locks to gain unauthorized access.

Example Attack Scenario:

An ethical hacker **dresses as a delivery worker** and walks into a corporate office carrying a package. They **tailgate an employee through a secured entrance**, bypassing security protocols and gaining physical access to restricted areas.

4.3 Penetration Testing Methodologies and Frameworks

Penetration testing follows **industry-recognized methodologies** to ensure structured and effective security assessments.

4.3.1 NIST Penetration Testing Methodology

The **National Institute of Standards and Technology (NIST)** provides a **standardized penetration testing framework** to help organizations conduct structured security assessments.
   NIST Penetration Testing Steps:

1. **Planning:** Define objectives, scope, and testing boundaries.
2. **Discovery:** Gather intelligence through reconnaissance and scanning.
3. **Attack:** Exploit vulnerabilities to test security defenses.
4. **Reporting:** Document findings and remediation recommendations.

4.3.2 OWASP Testing Guide (Web Application Security)

The **Open Web Application Security Project (OWASP)** provides a **comprehensive methodology for testing web applications**.
   Key OWASP Testing Areas:

- **Injection Attacks (SQLi, Command Injection).**
- **Authentication and Session Management Flaws.**
- **Security Misconfigurations and Data Exposure Risks.**

4.3.3 PTES (Penetration Testing Execution Standard)

The **Penetration Testing Execution Standard (PTES)** is a widely used framework that provides **a structured approach to penetration testing**.
   PTES Phases:

1. **Pre-engagement Interactions:** Define scope, objectives, and legal agreements.
2. **Intelligence Gathering:** Perform reconnaissance and scanning.
3. **Exploitation:** Attempt to gain access to systems.
4. **Post-Exploitation:** Establish persistence and elevate privileges.

5. **Reporting:** Document vulnerabilities and mitigation strategies.

4.4 Reporting and Post-Penetration Testing Activities

After completing a penetration test, **security teams must document findings and present actionable recommendations**.

Key Components of a Penetration Testing Report:

- **Executive Summary:** Overview of vulnerabilities and business risks.
- **Technical Findings:** Detailed description of exploited weaknesses.
- **Risk Assessment:** Severity ratings and potential impact analysis.
- **Mitigation Strategies:** Recommended security enhancements.

Post-Penetration Testing Best Practices:

- Conduct **remediation testing** to verify fixes.
- Implement **continuous security monitoring**.
- Provide **security awareness training** based on findings.

Conclusion

Penetration testing is an **essential cybersecurity practice** that helps organizations identify vulnerabilities before attackers exploit them. By following **structured methodologies, leveraging advanced tools, and conducting real-world attack simulations**, penetration testers play a **critical role in strengthening cybersecurity defenses**.

In **Chapter 5: Cyber Warfare and State-Sponsored Hacking**, we will explore **nation-state cyber threats, advanced persistent threats (APTs), and geopolitical cyber conflicts that shape modern cybersecurity challenges**.

Chapter 5

CYBER WARFARE AND STATE-SPONSORED HACKING

5.1 Introduction to Cyber Warfare

Cyber warfare is the **use of digital attacks by nations, state-sponsored groups, or military units to infiltrate, disrupt, or damage rival governments, critical infrastructure, and economic systems**. Unlike traditional warfare, cyber warfare operates in the **digital domain**, where adversaries target **power grids, banking systems, defense networks, intelligence agencies, and election processes** without deploying physical military forces.

Cyber warfare has become a **primary weapon in modern geopolitical conflicts**, with governments developing **offensive cyber capabilities** to achieve military, political, and economic objectives. Nations invest heavily in **offensive cyber operations, cyber intelligence, and cyber espionage programs** to undermine their adversaries, steal classified data, and influence global events.

Understanding cyber warfare is essential for **governments, cybersecurity professionals, and businesses**, as digital conflict continues to shape the modern world.

5.2 Understanding State-Sponsored Hacking

State-sponsored hacking refers to **cyber attacks carried out by government-backed groups to infiltrate, spy on, disrupt, or sabotage foreign entities**. These attacks are often **highly sophisticated and persistent**, leveraging advanced hacking tools, **zero-day vulnerabilities, and artificial intelligence**.

Objectives of State-Sponsored Hacking:

1. **Espionage:** Gaining unauthorized access to **government, military, and corporate networks** to steal classified intelligence.
2. **Infrastructure Sabotage:** Targeting **power grids, water supplies, financial systems, and nuclear facilities** to cause widespread disruption.
3. **Disinformation Campaigns:** Spreading false information to **manipulate elections, destabilize societies, and influence political decisions**.
4. **Intellectual Property Theft:** Stealing **scientific, technological, and military research** to gain a competitive advantage.
5. **Economic Warfare:** Launching cyber attacks against **banks, stock markets, and major industries** to weaken rival economies.

Characteristics of State-Sponsored Attacks:

- **Advanced Persistent Threats (APTs):** Multi-stage, stealthy cyber campaigns conducted over months or years.
- **Zero-Day Exploits:** Using undiscovered vulnerabilities to bypass security defenses.
- **Custom Malware and Backdoors:** Developing sophisticated cyber weapons that evade traditional antivirus tools.
- **Coordination with Intelligence Agencies:** State-sponsored hackers operate alongside military intelligence divisions.

These cyber operations **rarely leave clear traces**, making attribution difficult and allowing states to **deny involvement** in cyber warfare activities.

5.3 Major State-Sponsored Cyber Units

Several nations maintain **highly advanced cyber warfare divisions** that conduct intelligence operations, cyber espionage, and digital sabotage campaigns. These units operate under different **military, intelligence, and governmental agencies** worldwide.

United States – U.S. Cyber Command (USCYBERCOM)

- Oversees **offensive and defensive cyber operations**.
- Conducts **cyber defense for the U.S. military and intelligence networks**.
- Launched **Stuxnet (with Israeli cooperation) against Iran's nuclear program**.

Russia – GRU Unit 26165 (Fancy Bear) and FSB-linked hacking groups

- Conducts **cyber espionage, election interference, and intelligence operations**.
- Infiltrated **Ukraine's power grid in 2015, causing massive blackouts**.
- Responsible for the **SolarWinds supply chain attack in 2020**.

China – People's Liberation Army (PLA) Strategic Support Force

- Focuses on **industrial espionage, cyber theft, and political disinformation**.
- Conducted large-scale attacks on **U.S. defense contractors and technology firms**.
- Stole **data on 21 million individuals from the U.S. Office of Personnel Management in 2015**.

North Korea – Lazarus Group

- Specializes in **financial cybercrime, ransomware, and cryptocurrency theft**.
- Launched the **2017 WannaCry ransomware attack, affecting 200,000 computers worldwide**.
- Stole **$81 million from the Bank of Bangladesh in a sophisticated cyber heist**.

Iran – APT33 and APT34

- Engages in **cyber warfare against U.S., Israel, and Saudi Arabia**.
- Conducts **attacks on energy sectors, financial institutions, and infrastructure**.
- In 2012, wiped **30,000 computers belonging to Saudi Aramco using Shamoon malware**.

These cyber units are **constantly engaged in intelligence operations, data theft, and cyber sabotage**, shaping modern cyber warfare strategies.

5.4 Advanced Persistent Threats (APTs) in Cyber Warfare

An **Advanced Persistent Threat (APT)** is a **long-term, stealthy cyber attack designed to infiltrate high-value targets and remain undetected for extended periods**. APTs are typically **backed by nation-states or highly organized cybercriminal groups**.

Common Techniques Used in APT Attacks:

1. **Social Engineering and Phishing Attacks:** Trick high-level employees into revealing credentials.
2. **Zero-Day Exploits:** Attack undiscovered software vulnerabilities.
3. **Stealth Malware Deployment:** Deploy rootkits, keyloggers, and custom

malware.

4. **Command and Control (C2) Infrastructure:** Maintain persistent access to compromised systems.
5. **Lateral Movement:** Spread across networks to exfiltrate sensitive data.

Real-World APT Examples:

- **APT29 (Cozy Bear) – Russia:** Linked to the **2020 SolarWinds breach, which compromised U.S. government agencies**.
- **APT10 (China) – Cloud Hopper Attack:** Infiltrated **global IT providers and exfiltrated data from Fortune 500 companies**.
- **APT38 (North Korea) – Financial Attacks:** Stole **hundreds of millions from financial institutions worldwide**.

APTs **pose long-term threats** as they operate **covertly**, making them **one of the most dangerous cyber threats today**.

5.5 Cyber Weapons and Military-Grade Malware

Nation-states develop **custom cyber weapons and military-grade malware** to disrupt infrastructure, compromise security, and conduct espionage. These cyber weapons **can cripple power grids, disrupt financial institutions, and destroy critical systems**.

Notorious Cyber Weapons:

- **Stuxnet (2010):**First known cyber weapon targeting **Iran's nuclear centrifuges**.
- Caused **physical destruction** of industrial equipment.
- **NotPetya (2017):**Designed to **cripple Ukrainian businesses and infrastructure**.
- Caused **$10 billion in damages worldwide**, affecting multinational corporations.

- **Industroyer (2016):**Used by **Russia to disrupt Ukraine's power grid**, leading to **mass blackouts**.

Cyber weapons are **rapidly evolving**, making **cyber defense critical for national security**.

5.6 Defending Against State-Sponsored Attacks

Organizations, governments, and individuals must adopt **proactive cybersecurity strategies** to defend against **nation-state cyber threats**.

Key Defense Strategies:

1. **Threat Intelligence Sharing:** Collaborate with government agencies and cybersecurity firms.
2. **Zero Trust Security Model:** Assume **no user or system is inherently trusted**.
3. **Advanced Endpoint Detection and Response (EDR):** Monitor and neutralize APT activities.
4. **Air-Gapped Networks:** Protect **critical infrastructure from remote cyber attacks**.
5. **Multi-Factor Authentication (MFA):** Reduce the impact of credential theft.
6. **Regular Cybersecurity Training:** Equip employees to recognize **phishing and social engineering attacks**.

Conclusion

Cyber warfare and state-sponsored hacking **have redefined global conflict**, making **digital security as crucial as physical military strength**. As cyber weapons become more advanced, **governments and cybersecurity professionals must develop stronger defense strategies** to protect infrastructure, economies, and critical data from cyber espionage and sabotage.

In **Chapter 6: Cryptography and Secure Communications**, we will explore **encryption techniques, cryptographic algorithms, and secure communication protocols** that form the foundation of **modern cybersecurity** and **data protection**.

Chapter 6

CRYPTOGRAPHY AND SECURE COMMUNICATIONS

6.1 Introduction to Cryptography

Cryptography is the **science of securing information through mathematical techniques, encryption, and secure communication protocols**. It is a fundamental pillar of cybersecurity, ensuring **data confidentiality, integrity, authentication, and non-repudiation**.

With the rise of **cyber espionage, data breaches, and surveillance**, cryptographic systems are essential in **protecting sensitive data, securing communications, and safeguarding critical infrastructure** from cyber threats. Modern cryptography is used in **banking transactions, secure messaging, blockchain technology, digital signatures, and military communications**.

Understanding cryptographic principles is essential for **cybersecurity professionals, ethical hackers, and security architects** in building secure digital systems that withstand attacks from cybercriminals, state-sponsored hackers, and advanced persistent threats.

6.2 The Core Principles of Cryptography

Cryptographic security relies on **four primary principles** that ensure digital data remains secure from unauthorized access and tampering.

6.2.1 Confidentiality

Confidentiality ensures that **only authorized users can access sensitive data**. Encryption techniques such as **Advanced Encryption Standard (AES)** protect information by making it unreadable to anyone without the correct decryption key.
   Example:

 · A **bank encrypts customer financial records** before storing them in its database to prevent unauthorized access in case of a breach.

6.2.2 Integrity

Integrity guarantees that **data remains unaltered during transmission or storage**. Cryptographic hash functions such as **SHA-256** detect **unauthorized modifications** by generating a unique fingerprint for each dataset.
   Example:

 · Digital forensics teams use **hash values** to verify that collected evidence remains untampered throughout an investigation.

6.2.3 Authentication

Authentication verifies the **identity of users and devices** in a system using **digital certificates, passwords, and biometric authentication**. Secure authentication methods prevent **unauthorized access and identity fraud**.
   Example:

 · Websites use **SSL/TLS certificates** to verify that users are communicating with the real server and not a fake phishing site.

6.2.4 Non-Repudiation

Non-repudiation ensures that **a sender cannot deny sending a message, and a receiver cannot deny receiving it**. Digital signatures and blockchain-based transaction logs provide cryptographic proof of digital interactions.
  Example:

- A **CEO digitally signs an electronic contract**, ensuring that the document is legally binding and verifiable.

Cryptography relies on these principles to **secure data, prevent cyber threats, and establish trust in digital transactions**.

6.3 Types of Cryptographic Algorithms

Cryptographic security relies on various mathematical algorithms designed to **encrypt, decrypt, and authenticate information securely**. These algorithms are classified into three main categories:

6.3.1 Symmetric Encryption (Private Key Cryptography)

Symmetric encryption uses **a single key** to encrypt and decrypt data. It is **fast and efficient** but requires **secure key distribution** between parties.
  Common Symmetric Encryption Algorithms:

- **AES (Advanced Encryption Standard):** Used in government and military applications for securing classified information.
- **DES (Data Encryption Standard):** A legacy encryption standard that has been replaced due to vulnerabilities.
- **Blowfish:** Used in VPN encryption and secure file storage.

Example:

- A **corporation encrypts its employee database using AES-256**, ensuring that only authorized personnel can access it.

6.3.2 Asymmetric Encryption (Public Key Cryptography)

Asymmetric encryption uses **a pair of keys: a public key and a private key**. Data encrypted with a **public key** can only be decrypted with its corresponding **private key**, and vice versa.
   Common Asymmetric Encryption Algorithms:

- **RSA (Rivest-Shamir-Adleman):** Used in SSL/TLS certificates, digital signatures, and secure email communication.
- **ECC (Elliptic Curve Cryptography):** Provides stronger security with shorter key lengths, making it ideal for mobile devices and IoT security.
- **Diffie-Hellman Key Exchange:** Enables secure key distribution over an insecure network.

Example:

- **Email encryption systems use RSA keys** to ensure that only the intended recipient can read a message.

6.3.3 Hash Functions

Cryptographic hash functions generate **fixed-length unique fingerprints (hashes) for data**. Hashes are **irreversible** and provide **data integrity verification**.
   Common Cryptographic Hash Functions:

- **SHA-256 (Secure Hash Algorithm):** Used in Bitcoin transactions and digital certificates.
- **MD5 (Message Digest Algorithm 5):** Previously used for password hashing but is now considered weak due to collision attacks.

- **Bcrypt:** Designed for securely hashing passwords with built-in **salting** to prevent brute-force attacks.

Example:

- **Blockchain networks use SHA-256 hashing** to verify transactions and prevent data tampering.

6.4 Cryptography in Secure Communications

Secure communication protocols rely on cryptographic techniques to **protect data from interception, tampering, and unauthorized access**. These protocols ensure **safe online transactions, encrypted messaging, and private browsing**.

6.4.1 SSL/TLS – Secure Sockets Layer / Transport Layer Security

SSL/TLS secures **web traffic between browsers and servers**, encrypting sensitive information such as **login credentials, credit card details, and online communications**.
   How SSL/TLS Works:

1. **The client (web browser) initiates a secure connection.**
2. **The server provides an SSL/TLS certificate signed by a trusted authority.**
3. **A cryptographic key exchange secures communication between the client and the server.**
4. **All transmitted data is encrypted, preventing eavesdropping and man-in-the-middle attacks.**

Example:

- **Banking websites use TLS encryption** to protect customer transactions from cybercriminals.

6.4.2 End-to-End Encryption (E2EE)

End-to-end encryption ensures that **only the sender and recipient can decrypt messages**, preventing third-party access.
   Popular End-to-End Encrypted Messaging Apps:

- **Signal:** Uses the Signal Protocol for encrypted messaging and calls.
- **WhatsApp:** Implements **E2EE for text, voice, and video communication**.
- **ProtonMail:** Provides **secure, encrypted email services**.

Example:

- **Journalists use end-to-end encrypted messaging apps** to protect their communications from government surveillance.

6.4.3 Virtual Private Networks (VPNs)

VPNs create **encrypted tunnels between users and remote servers**, hiding IP addresses and encrypting internet traffic.
   Benefits of Using a VPN:

- Prevents **internet service providers from tracking browsing activity**.
- Bypasses **geographical restrictions and censorship**.
- Secures data transmission on **public Wi-Fi networks**.

Example:

- A **corporate executive traveling abroad uses a VPN** to securely access company servers without exposing confidential information.

6.5 Quantum Computing and the Future of Cryptography

Quantum computing poses a **major threat to cryptographic security** by **potentially breaking traditional encryption algorithms** through quantum decryption techniques.

Potential Risks of Quantum Computing:

- **Shor's Algorithm:** Can break RSA and ECC encryption, rendering current public-key cryptography obsolete.
- **Grover's Algorithm:** Reduces the time needed for brute-force attacks on cryptographic keys.

Post-Quantum Cryptography (PQC):

To defend against quantum threats, researchers are developing **quantum-resistant encryption techniques**, including:

- **Lattice-based cryptography.**
- **Multivariate polynomial cryptography.**
- **Hash-based signature schemes.**

Organizations must **prepare for the quantum era by transitioning to quantum-resistant cryptographic systems** to ensure long-term security.

Conclusion

Cryptography is **essential in modern cybersecurity**, protecting data, securing communication channels, and ensuring digital privacy. With evolving threats such as **nation-state cyber espionage, artificial intelligence-driven attacks, and quantum computing**, organizations must adopt **advanced cryptographic techniques** to safeguard sensitive information.

In **Chapter 7: Malware Analysis and Threat Intelligence**, we will explore how cybersecurity professionals analyze malware, detect cyber threats, and develop countermeasures to mitigate cyber attacks.

Chapter 7

MALWARE ANALYSIS AND THREAT INTELLIGENCE

7.1 Introduction to Malware Analysis

Malware analysis is the **process of examining malicious software to understand its behavior, functionality, and impact**. Security researchers, penetration testers, and incident response teams analyze malware to **develop countermeasures, detect infections, and prevent future attacks**.

Malware threats are **constantly evolving**, employing **polymorphism, encryption, and obfuscation techniques** to evade detection. Modern cybersecurity strategies depend on **reverse engineering malware, analyzing its code, and developing signatures for antivirus and endpoint protection systems**.

Malware analysis plays a crucial role in **threat intelligence**, where security professionals **track cybercriminal groups, attribute attacks to specific threat actors, and anticipate new cyber threats before they emerge**.

7.2 Categories of Malware

Malware is classified based on its **behavior, propagation method, and impact on infected systems**. Understanding these categories is essential for **detecting, analyzing, and mitigating malicious software**.

7.2.1 Viruses

A **virus** is a self-replicating program that attaches itself to legitimate files and **requires user interaction to execute and spread**.
Characteristics of Viruses:

- Modify or corrupt system files.
- Spread through **email attachments, software downloads, and infected USB drives**.
- Often disguised as **legitimate applications**.

Example:

- The **ILOVEYOU virus (2000)** spread through email attachments, infecting millions of computers worldwide and causing **billions in damages**.

7.2.2 Worms

A **worm** is a type of malware that spreads autonomously **without user interaction**, exploiting **network vulnerabilities and misconfigurations**.
Characteristics of Worms:

- Self-replicating and spreads rapidly across systems.
- Targets **unpatched software vulnerabilities**.
- Often used in **botnets for launching distributed denial-of-service (DDoS) attacks**.

Example:

- The **WannaCry ransomware worm (2017)** exploited **EternalBlue (MS17-010)** in Windows systems, infecting over **230,000 computers worldwide**.

7.2.3 Trojans

A **trojan horse** is a form of malware that **disguises itself as legitimate software** while secretly executing **malicious operations**.

Types of Trojans:

- **Remote Access Trojans (RATs):** Allow attackers to **control infected systems remotely**.
- **Banking Trojans:** Steal **financial credentials and credit card information**.
- **Backdoor Trojans:** Create **hidden access points** for persistent attacks.

Example:

- The **Emotet banking trojan** infected thousands of financial institutions, enabling **credential theft and fraud**.

7.2.4 Ransomware

Ransomware encrypts a victim's files and demands payment for decryption keys, often requiring payment in **cryptocurrency**.

Common Ransomware Attack Strategies:

- **Double Extortion:** Attackers steal data before encryption and threaten to **leak sensitive information** if the ransom is not paid.
- **Ransomware-as-a-Service (RaaS):** Cybercriminal groups sell ransomware toolkits to affiliates.
- **Targeted Attacks on Critical Infrastructure:** Hospitals, financial institutions, and **government agencies** are primary targets.

Example:

- The **Colonial Pipeline ransomware attack (2021)** caused **fuel shortages**

across the U.S. East Coast, forcing the company to **pay $4.4 million in Bitcoin** to regain access.

7.2.5 Spyware and Keyloggers

Spyware secretly monitors user activity, capturing keystrokes, browsing history, and sensitive data.
  Spyware Attack Techniques:

- **Keylogging:** Records every keystroke to capture **passwords and confidential data**.
- **Screen Capturing:** Takes periodic screenshots of victim activity.
- **Clipboard Hijacking:** Monitors and replaces copied data, often targeting **cryptocurrency wallet addresses**.

Example:

- The **Agent Tesla keylogger** is commonly used in **corporate espionage** and **nation-state cyber attacks**.

7.2.6 Rootkits

Rootkits provide attackers with **privileged access to a system**, allowing them to **hide malware, disable security tools, and evade detection**.
  Rootkit Capabilities:

- **Kernel-Level Manipulation:** Modifies core operating system processes.
- **Process Injection:** Embeds malicious code into **legitimate system processes**.
- **Persistence Mechanisms:** Survives reboots and security updates.

Example:

- The **Sony BMG rootkit (2005)** was discovered in **music CDs** that secretly installed software to prevent piracy but also introduced **security vulnerabilities**.

7.3 Malware Analysis Techniques

Security researchers analyze malware using **static, dynamic, and behavioral analysis techniques** to understand its functionality and develop countermeasures.

7.3.1 Static Analysis

Static analysis involves **examining malware code without executing it** to detect **potential threats and vulnerabilities**.
Static Analysis Techniques:

- **Signature-Based Detection:** Compares malware code with known signatures in antivirus databases.
- **Strings Analysis:** Extracts readable text and API calls from **executable files**.
- **PE Header Inspection:** Examines **Portable Executable (PE) file structures** to identify anomalies.

Tools Used in Static Analysis:

- **PEiD:** Detects packers, encryptors, and compilers used in malware.
- **Binwalk:** Analyzes embedded files within executables.
- **YARA Rules:** Defines patterns for identifying malware families.

7.3.2 Dynamic Analysis

Dynamic analysis involves **executing malware in a controlled environment** (sandbox) to observe **real-time behavior, network activity, and system modifications**.
   Dynamic Analysis Techniques:

- **Process Monitoring:** Tracks **system calls, registry modifications, and network connections**.
- **Network Traffic Analysis:** Identifies **command-and-control (C2) communications**.
- **Memory Forensics:** Analyzes active processes to detect **hidden payloads and encryption routines**.

Tools Used in Dynamic Analysis:

- **Cuckoo Sandbox:** Executes malware in a virtualized environment.
- **Wireshark:** Captures and inspects malicious network traffic.
- **Volatility Framework:** Performs **live memory forensics on infected systems**.

7.4 Threat Intelligence and Malware Attribution

Threat intelligence involves **collecting, analyzing, and correlating cyber threat data** to predict and prevent attacks.

Sources of Threat Intelligence:

- **Dark Web Monitoring:** Tracks cybercriminal marketplaces for emerging threats.
- **Threat Feeds:** Government and private cybersecurity firms share **real-time attack indicators (IOCs)**.
- **Honeypots:** Deceptive systems designed to lure attackers and study

malware behaviors.

7.5 Malware Countermeasures and Defense Strategies

Organizations must implement **proactive security measures** to prevent malware infections and mitigate cyber attacks.

Best Practices for Malware Defense:

- **Implement Zero Trust Security:** Assume **all systems and users are potential threats**.
- **Use Endpoint Detection and Response (EDR):** Monitors and neutralizes threats in real-time.
- **Regular Patch Management:** Prevents exploits by keeping software up to date.
- **Security Awareness Training:** Educates employees to recognize phishing and social engineering attempts.
- **Application Whitelisting:** Restricts execution to **approved software only**.

Advanced Protection Technologies:

- **AI-Powered Threat Detection:** Identifies malware **using machine learning models**.
- **Blockchain Security Protocols:** Ensures **tamper-proof data integrity**.
- **Quantum-Resistant Encryption:** Protects against **future quantum computing attacks**.

Conclusion

Malware is a **significant cybersecurity threat**, constantly evolving to bypass detection mechanisms. Through **comprehensive malware analysis, threat intelligence, and proactive defense strategies**, organizations can **mitigate risks, detect cyber threats, and strengthen security measures**.

In **Chapter 8: Security Operations and Incident Response**, we will explore how cybersecurity teams respond to cyber incidents, contain malware outbreaks, and conduct forensic investigations to identify attack origins and prevent future intrusions.

Chapter 8

SECURITY OPERATIONS AND INCIDENT RESPONSE

8.1 Introduction to Security Operations

Security operations encompass **the continuous monitoring, detection, and response to cybersecurity threats** in an organization's digital environment. The **Security Operations Center (SOC)** serves as the central hub for **cyber threat analysis, intrusion detection, and incident response coordination**.

Organizations face a constant **onslaught of cyber threats, including ransomware, phishing attacks, insider threats, and nation-state cyber espionage**. Without an effective security operations strategy, organizations remain vulnerable to data breaches, financial losses, and reputational damage.

Security operations integrate **threat intelligence, security automation, forensic analysis, and incident response methodologies** to detect and neutralize cyber threats before they cause significant harm.

8.2 The Role of a Security Operations Center (SOC)

A **Security Operations Center (SOC)** is a **dedicated team of cybersecurity professionals** responsible for protecting an organization's digital assets from cyber threats. SOC teams **monitor networks, analyze threat intelligence, respond to incidents, and implement cybersecurity policies**.

8.2.1 Key Responsibilities of a SOC

- **Continuous Threat Monitoring:** Uses **Security Information and Event Management (SIEM)** tools to detect **anomalies and malicious activity** in real-time.
- **Incident Detection and Response:** Identifies **ongoing cyber attacks** and coordinates **rapid response efforts**.
- **Threat Intelligence Integration:** Analyzes **Indicators of Compromise (IOCs)** and **Tactics, Techniques, and Procedures (TTPs)** used by cyber-criminals.
- **Vulnerability Management:** Regularly scans systems for **security flaws and misconfigurations**.
- **Digital Forensics and Post-Incident Analysis:** Investigates security breaches to determine **attack origins, methods, and potential damage**.

8.2.2 SOC Team Roles and Responsibilities

SOC teams are structured into different roles based on **expertise and responsibilities**:

SOC Role	Primary Responsibilities
SOC Analyst (Tier 1-3)	Monitors security alerts, investigates incidents, and escalates critical threats.
Incident Responder	Coordinates rapid response to security breaches and malware outbreaks.
Threat Intelligence Analyst	Tracks cybercriminal activities, analyzes attack patterns, and predicts emerging threats.
Forensic Investigator	Conducts post-incident forensic analysis to reconstruct cyber attacks.
SOC Manager	Oversees SOC operations, enforces security policies, and reports incidents to executives.

SOC teams play a **critical role in cybersecurity defense**, ensuring that **threats are detected and mitigated before they escalate into full-scale cyber incidents**.

8.3 The Cybersecurity Incident Response Lifecycle

Incident response is a **structured approach for handling cybersecurity incidents, minimizing damage, and restoring normal operations**. The **National Institute of Standards and Technology (NIST) Incident Response Framework** defines a **four-phase approach** for incident response.

8.3.1 Phase 1: Preparation

Organizations must develop a **comprehensive incident response plan (IRP)** to ensure that security teams can respond **efficiently** to cyber threats.
Preparation Best Practices:

- Establish **Incident Response Teams (IRT)** with defined roles and responsibilities.
- Develop **response playbooks** for different attack scenarios.
- Conduct **tabletop exercises** to simulate cyber attack scenarios and test response strategies.
- Deploy **SIEM solutions** to centralize log data for real-time threat detection.

8.3.2 Phase 2: Detection and Analysis

During this phase, **SOC analysts and security tools identify suspicious activity and classify security incidents**.
Indicators of Compromise (IOCs):

- **Unusual network traffic spikes** indicating a **DDoS attack**.
- **Unauthorized access attempts** on privileged accounts.
- **Malware signatures detected** in system logs.
- **Anomalous file modifications**, signaling **ransomware activity**.

Detection Tools:

- **SIEM Solutions (Splunk, IBM QRadar, ArcSight):** Aggregates and analyzes security logs for anomaly detection.
- **Intrusion Detection Systems (Snort, Suricata):** Detects malicious network activity.
- **Endpoint Detection and Response (EDR) Platforms:** Monitors **endpoint behavior and prevents malware execution**.

Once an incident is detected, analysts **determine its severity, affected systems, and potential impact** before escalating the case to the **Incident Response Team (IRT)**.

8.3.3 Phase 3: Containment, Eradication, and Recovery

Once a cyber attack is confirmed, the **primary objective is to limit damage, remove the threat, and restore affected systems**.
   Containment Strategies:

- **Network Segmentation:** Isolate infected systems to prevent malware propagation.
- **Account Lockdowns:** Disable compromised user accounts to prevent unauthorized access.
- **Traffic Filtering:** Block malicious IP addresses using **firewall and intrusion prevention systems (IPS)**.

Eradication Strategies:

- **Removing Malware:** Use **EDR solutions** to detect and remove persistent threats.
- **Patching Vulnerabilities:** Apply **security updates** to prevent reinfection.
- **Credential Resetting:** Enforce **password resets and multi-factor authentication (MFA)**.

Recovery Strategies:

- Restore systems from **clean backups**.
- Conduct **penetration testing** to verify security posture.
- Implement **continuous monitoring** to detect any residual threats.

8.3.4 Phase 4: Post-Incident Analysis and Reporting

After an incident is resolved, organizations must conduct a **post-mortem analysis** to improve future security strategies.
   Key Components of a Post-Incident Report:

- **Incident Summary:** Overview of attack type, affected systems, and impact.
- **Attack Vector Analysis:** How the attack originated and exploited vulnerabilities.
- **Response Effectiveness:** Evaluation of containment and mitigation strategies.
- **Recommendations:** Security enhancements to prevent recurrence.

By analyzing past incidents, security teams can **strengthen their defenses and improve incident response readiness**.

8.4 Cyber Threat Hunting and Proactive Defense

Traditional cybersecurity strategies **rely on reactive measures**, but **threat hunting focuses on proactively identifying hidden cyber threats** before they execute attacks.

8.4.1 Threat Hunting Methodologies

- **Hypothesis-Driven Threat Hunting:** Investigates **potential attack patterns** based on historical data.
- **Behavioral Analytics:** Uses **machine learning models** to detect anomalies in network activity.

- **Adversary Emulation:** Simulates attacks using **red teaming exercises** to test security defenses.

Threat Hunting Tools:

- **MITRE ATT&CK Framework:** Maps adversary tactics and techniques.
- **Sysmon (Windows Event Logging):** Monitors system processes for suspicious behavior.
- **ELK Stack (Elasticsearch, Logstash, Kibana):** Aggregates log data for real-time threat analysis.

Proactive **threat hunting strengthens security operations**, ensuring **attackers are identified and neutralized before they breach systems**.

8.5 Security Automation and Artificial Intelligence in Incident Response

Modern cybersecurity operations leverage **automation and artificial intelligence (AI) to enhance incident response speed and efficiency**.

8.5.1 Security Orchestration, Automation, and Response (SOAR)

SOAR platforms **automate threat detection, investigation, and response** to reduce **manual workloads for SOC analysts**.
  SOAR Capabilities:

- **Automated Incident Triage:** Classifies alerts based on severity.
- **Threat Intelligence Correlation:** Analyzes attack patterns in real time.
- **Automated Remediation:** Blocks malicious traffic and quarantines infected systems.

8.5.2 AI-Powered Cyber Defense

- **Machine Learning-Based Anomaly Detection:** Identifies deviations from normal behavior.
- **Automated Malware Analysis:** Uses AI to classify **new malware strains**.
- **Predictive Threat Intelligence:** Detects **emerging cyber threats** before they materialize.

By integrating **AI-driven automation**, security operations **become more efficient, responsive, and adaptive to evolving cyber threats**.

Conclusion

Security operations and incident response are **critical components of modern cybersecurity defense**. By implementing **advanced monitoring systems, effective threat intelligence strategies, and AI-driven automation**, organizations can **detect, respond to, and prevent cyber attacks in real time**.

In **Chapter 9: Defensive Cybersecurity Strategies**, we will explore **cyber resilience planning, zero-trust architectures, endpoint security measures, and advanced defense techniques for modern cybersecurity threats**.

Chapter 9

DEFENSIVE CYBERSECURITY STRATEGIES

9.1 Introduction to Cyber Defense

Cyber defense refers to **proactive and reactive security measures implemented to protect digital assets, networks, applications, and data from cyber threats**. Organizations must adopt **multi-layered defense strategies** to mitigate risks posed by **ransomware, phishing attacks, insider threats, advanced persistent threats (APTs), and state-sponsored cyber warfare**.

Effective cybersecurity defense strategies **prioritize prevention, detection, response, and recovery**, ensuring resilience against modern cyber adversaries. This chapter explores **advanced cybersecurity frameworks, zero-trust security models, endpoint security measures, and cyber resilience planning**.

9.2 The Cybersecurity Defense-in-Depth Strategy

Defense-in-depth is a **multi-layered cybersecurity strategy** that incorporates **several security controls across an organization's digital infrastructure**. Rather than relying on a **single security mechanism**, this approach ensures that **multiple protective layers mitigate various attack vectors**.

9.2.1 Key Layers of Defense-in-Depth

Defense Layer	Security Mechanism	Purpose
Perimeter Security	Firewalls, Intrusion Detection Systems (IDS), Intrusion Prevention Systems (IPS)	Blocks unauthorized access and detects anomalies.
Network Security	Network segmentation, VPNs, Zero Trust Architecture	Controls access and restricts lateral movement.
Endpoint Security	Endpoint Detection and Response (EDR), Antivirus, Application Whitelisting	Protects individual devices from malware and unauthorized access.
Identity and Access Management (IAM)	Multi-Factor Authentication (MFA), Privileged Access Management (PAM)	Enforces authentication and access control policies.
Data Security	Encryption, Data Loss Prevention (DLP), Cloud Security Controls	Ensures confidentiality and integrity of sensitive data.
Security Awareness Training	Phishing Simulations, Social Engineering Defense	Educates users on cyber threats and best practices.

A **layered defense approach** ensures that if **one security measure fails, another compensates**, reducing the likelihood of successful cyber intrusions.

9.3 The Zero Trust Security Model

Zero Trust is a **modern cybersecurity framework** based on the principle that **no user, device, or network should be trusted by default**. Unlike traditional perimeter-based security models, Zero Trust enforces **continuous authentication, access control, and network segmentation**.

9.3.1 Core Principles of Zero Trust Security

1. **Verify Every User and Device:** Requires **multi-factor authentication (MFA), biometric verification, and device authentication**.
2. **Enforce Least Privilege Access:** Limits user access to **only necessary data and resources**.
3. **Micro-Segmentation:** Divides networks into **isolated security zones** to

prevent lateral movement of attackers.

4. **Continuous Monitoring:** Uses **behavioral analytics and machine learning to detect anomalies**.

5. **Encrypt Data at Rest and in Transit:** Ensures **confidentiality of sensitive information**.

Example Implementation:

- A **Zero Trust framework** ensures that even **internal employees** must re-authenticate before accessing high-value data repositories.

Organizations that **implement Zero Trust architectures** reduce their attack surface, preventing **insider threats, unauthorized access, and advanced cyber attacks**.

9.4 Endpoint Security and Next-Generation Defense Mechanisms

Endpoints, including **laptops, mobile devices, servers, and IoT devices**, are **primary attack vectors** for cybercriminals. Organizations must **deploy endpoint security solutions** to protect against **ransomware, malware, and unauthorized access**.

9.4.1 Advanced Endpoint Security Technologies

1. **Endpoint Detection and Response (EDR):**

- Detects **real-time malware infections and unauthorized activities**.
- Uses **machine learning to analyze behavior patterns**.

1. **Extended Detection and Response (XDR):**

- Correlates security data across **endpoints, networks, cloud environments, and applications**.

- Provides **automated incident response and remediation**.

1. **Next-Generation Antivirus (NGAV):**

- Detects threats using **artificial intelligence (AI) rather than traditional signature-based detection**.
- Prevents **fileless malware, polymorphic viruses, and script-based attacks**.

1. **Application Whitelisting and Sandboxing:**

- Ensures only **trusted applications can execute** on systems.
- Isolates **suspicious files in a controlled environment** for analysis.

Example Implementation:

- A **global financial institution deploys EDR and XDR solutions** to detect and prevent **malware-based financial fraud attempts** in real time.

9.5 Threat Intelligence and Proactive Defense

Threat intelligence enables organizations to **anticipate and prevent cyber attacks** by analyzing cybercriminal tactics, techniques, and procedures (TTPs).

9.5.1 Threat Intelligence Sources

- **Dark Web Monitoring:** Tracks underground forums for leaked credentials and cybercriminal discussions.
- **Government Cybersecurity Agencies:** Organizations like **CISA, NSA, and INTERPOL share cyber threat intelligence**.
- **Commercial Threat Intelligence Feeds:** Security vendors provide **real-time attack indicators (IOCs)**.

· **Honeypots and Deception Technology:** Simulates vulnerable systems to **study attacker behaviors**.

9.5.2 Cyber Threat Intelligence Platforms (TIPs)

Threat intelligence platforms aggregate security data from **multiple sources, providing real-time analysis and automated threat detection**.
   Example Platforms:

· **IBM X-Force Exchange**
· **FireEye Helix**
· **Recorded Future Threat Intelligence**

Organizations that **leverage threat intelligence** gain **early warnings on emerging cyber threats, preventing zero-day attacks and targeted cyber intrusions**.

9.6 Cyber Resilience and Business Continuity Planning

Cyber resilience refers to an organization's **ability to withstand, adapt to, and recover from cyber attacks**.

9.6.1 Developing a Cyber Resilience Strategy

1. **Incident Response Planning:** Prepares teams for **real-time cyber threat mitigation**.
2. **Backup and Disaster Recovery (BDR):** Ensures **critical systems and data can be restored after a cyber attack**.
3. **Cyber Insurance Coverage:** Mitigates **financial risks associated with ransomware and data breaches**.
4. **Continuous Security Testing:** Conducts **regular penetration testing and vulnerability assessments**.

- **Red Team vs. Blue Team Exercises:Red Teams:** Simulate cyber attacks to test defenses.
- **Blue Teams:** Defend against simulated attacks and improve security controls.

9.7 Cloud Security and Hybrid Infrastructure Protection

As organizations transition to **cloud-based infrastructures**, security risks increase due to **misconfigured cloud environments, insider threats, and cloud-native cyber attacks**.

9.7.1 Cloud Security Best Practices

- **Implement Zero Trust Access Controls:** Restrict unauthorized access to cloud resources.
- **Secure Cloud Storage with Encryption:** Protect data stored in **AWS, Azure, and Google Cloud**.
- **Monitor Cloud Workloads for Anomalies:** Use **Cloud Security Posture Management (CSPM) tools**.
- **Deploy Cloud Workload Protection Platforms (CWPP):** Detects threats across **serverless applications and Kubernetes environments**.

Example Implementation:

- A **technology firm deploys multi-cloud security controls** to prevent unauthorized access to customer data stored in Amazon Web Services (AWS) and Google Cloud Platform (GCP).

Conclusion

Defensive cybersecurity strategies **require a combination of Zero Trust security models, endpoint protection, cloud security controls, and real-time threat intelligence**. Organizations that **implement multi-layered defense** architectures, leverage AI-powered cybersecurity tools, and maintain cyber resilience strategies remain protected against sophisticated cyber threats.

In **Chapter 10: Cybersecurity Governance, Risk, and Compliance**, we will explore **regulatory frameworks, risk management strategies, and industry compliance requirements for building secure and legally compliant cybersecurity programs.**

Chapter 10

CYBERSECURITY GOVERNANCE, RISK, AND COMPLIANCE

10.1 Introduction to Cybersecurity Governance

Cybersecurity governance establishes the **strategic framework, policies, and oversight mechanisms** required to **protect digital assets, ensure regulatory compliance, and manage cyber risks**. Organizations must implement **governance structures that define security responsibilities, enforce best practices, and align cybersecurity with business objectives**.

Effective cybersecurity governance integrates **risk management, legal compliance, incident response planning, and continuous security improvement** to protect against **cyber threats, financial losses, reputational damage, and legal liabilities**.

Cybersecurity governance is **not just a technical concern**; it requires **executive leadership, board oversight, and organizational-wide collaboration** to establish a **security-first culture**.

10.2 Governance Frameworks and Security Policies

Cybersecurity governance follows **internationally recognized frameworks** that provide **structured guidelines for managing security risks, implementing security controls, and ensuring regulatory compliance**.

10.2.1 Key Cybersecurity Governance Frameworks

Framework	Description	Use Case
NIST Cybersecurity Framework (CSF)	A risk-based approach to managing cybersecurity risks.	Used by U.S. government agencies and private sector organizations.
ISO/IEC 27001	International standard for information security management systems (ISMS).	Adopted by global enterprises and financial institutions.
CIS Controls	20 security controls to prevent, detect, and mitigate cyber threats.	Used by corporations, small businesses, and government agencies.
COBIT (Control Objectives for Information and Related Technologies)	Provides a governance model for aligning IT with business objectives.	Used by IT governance and risk management teams.

10.2.2 Essential Cybersecurity Policies

Organizations must define **comprehensive security policies** that outline **acceptable use, access control, data protection, and incident response protocols**.

Critical Cybersecurity Policies:

Acceptable Use Policy (AUP): Defines rules for **employee access to company systems and data**.

Data Classification Policy: Categorizes data based on **sensitivity and access controls**.

Access Control Policy: Implements **role-based access control (RBAC), least privilege principles, and multi-factor authentication (MFA)**.

Incident Response Policy: Establishes **guidelines for detecting, reporting, and responding to cyber incidents**.

Bring Your Own Device (BYOD) Policy: Regulates the **use of personal devices on corporate networks**.

Vendor Risk Management Policy: Assesses security risks associated with **third-party vendors and cloud service providers**.

A **well-defined governance framework and security policy structure** strengthen **organizational cybersecurity posture** and ensure compliance with industry regulations.

10.3 Cyber Risk Management and Threat Mitigation

Cyber risk management involves **identifying, analyzing, and mitigating security risks** that could impact **business operations, financial stability, and data protection**.

10.3.1 Cyber Risk Assessment Process

Identify Assets and Threats: Classify **critical IT infrastructure, cloud environments, and sensitive data repositories**.

Assess **potential cyber threats, including ransomware, insider threats, and supply chain attacks**.

Analyze Vulnerabilities: Conduct **penetration testing, vulnerability scanning, and red team exercises**.

Identify weaknesses in **firewalls, access controls, and endpoint security solutions**.

Evaluate Risk Impact and Likelihood: Determine the **business impact of cyber incidents, including financial losses and regulatory fines**.

Use **quantitative risk models** to prioritize remediation efforts.

Implement Risk Mitigation Strategies: Deploy **zero trust security models, encryption protocols, and threat intelligence platforms**.

Enhance **employee security awareness training and phishing simulations**.

Monitor and Review: Continuously assess security controls through **audit logs, SIEM monitoring, and real-time threat detection**.

Update risk mitigation strategies **as new threats emerge**.

By integrating **risk management into cybersecurity governance**, organizations can **proactively address threats, reduce vulnerabilities, and protect digital infrastructure from cyber attacks**.

10.4 Regulatory Compliance and Legal Requirements

Compliance with **cybersecurity regulations and data protection laws** is **mandatory for organizations handling sensitive information**. Non-compliance can result in **hefty fines, legal actions, and reputational damage**.

10.4.1 Major Cybersecurity Regulations and Data Privacy Laws

Regulation	Jurisdiction	Key Compliance Requirements
General Data Protection Regulation (GDPR)	European Union (EU)	Protects personal data and privacy rights of EU citizens.
California Consumer Privacy Act (CCPA)	United States (California)	Grants consumers rights over how their personal data is collected and shared.
Health Insurance Portability and Accountability Act (HIPAA)	United States	Regulates healthcare data privacy and security.
Payment Card Industry Data Security Standard (PCI-DSS)	Global	Establishes security requirements for processing credit card transactions.
Federal Information Security Modernization Act (FISMA)	United States	Requires federal agencies to maintain cybersecurity standards.

10.4.2 Compliance Best Practices

- Conduct **regular security audits and penetration testing** to verify compliance.
- Implement **strong data encryption and secure access controls**.
- Maintain **detailed cybersecurity documentation and incident response logs**.
- Appoint a **Data Protection Officer (DPO)** for organizations handling personal data.
- Train employees on **cybersecurity compliance requirements and legal responsibilities**.

Organizations that **adhere to compliance regulations** build **trust with customers, avoid regulatory fines, and strengthen cybersecurity defenses**.

10.5 Supply Chain Security and Third-Party Risk Management

Supply chain cyber attacks target **third-party vendors, cloud providers, and software supply chains** to infiltrate **larger organizations**.

10.5.1 Major Supply Chain Cyber Attacks

- **SolarWinds Breach (2020):** Nation-state hackers compromised **SolarWinds' software update**, infecting **U.S. government agencies and Fortune 500 companies**.
- **Kaseya Ransomware Attack (2021):** Attackers exploited **Kaseya's IT management platform**, deploying **ransomware to thousands of businesses worldwide**.

10.5.2 Best Practices for Supply Chain Security

- **Vendor Risk Assessments:** Evaluate **third-party cybersecurity controls** before onboarding vendors.
- **Zero Trust Access Controls:** Restrict **third-party access to critical systems**.
- **Software Bill of Materials (SBOM):** Maintain a **list of software components and dependencies** to detect vulnerabilities.
- **Continuous Security Monitoring:** Deploy **intrusion detection systems (IDS) and endpoint security solutions** for real-time threat detection.

Organizations must **fortify supply chain security** to prevent cybercriminals from exploiting **third-party vulnerabilities**.

10.6 Cybersecurity Audits and Continuous Compliance Monitoring

Regular cybersecurity audits ensure **compliance with industry regulations, identify security gaps, and enhance risk management strategies**.

10.6.1 Key Components of a Cybersecurity Audit

- **Penetration Testing:** Simulates **real-world cyber attacks** to assess security posture.
- **Vulnerability Assessments:** Identifies and remediates **security flaws in applications and network configurations**.
- **Log Analysis and Incident Reviews:** Analyzes **security event logs for suspicious activities**.
- **Regulatory Compliance Checks:** Verifies adherence to **GDPR, CCPA, PCI-DSS, and other cybersecurity laws**.

10.6.2 Continuous Compliance Monitoring Solutions

Organizations use **AI-driven security tools and SIEM platforms** to **automate compliance checks and detect policy violations**.
  Popular Compliance Monitoring Tools:

- **Splunk Enterprise Security** – Real-time security log analysis and compliance auditing.
- **Microsoft Compliance Manager** – Automates regulatory compliance tracking.
- **Qualys Cloud Security Assessment** – Identifies misconfigurations and compliance risks in cloud environments.

By **integrating compliance automation, conducting security audits, and enforcing governance frameworks**, organizations **ensure regulatory compliance and mitigate cybersecurity risks**.

Conclusion

Cybersecurity governance, risk management, and compliance are **foundational elements of a strong cybersecurity strategy**. Organizations that **adhere to security frameworks, enforce compliance standards, and integrate continuous risk assessments** maintain **resilience against evolving cyber threats**.

In **Chapter 11: Blockchain and Cryptocurrency Security**, we will explore **blockchain technology, cryptocurrency security risks, smart contract vulnerabilities, and decentralized finance (DeFi) cyber threats**.

Chapter 11

BLOCKCHAIN AND CRYPTOCURRENCY SECURITY

11.1 Introduction to Blockchain and Cryptocurrency Security

Blockchain technology underpins **cryptocurrencies, smart contracts, decentralized finance (DeFi), and digital identity systems**, offering **decentralization, immutability, and cryptographic security**. However, blockchain networks remain vulnerable to **cyber attacks, fraud, and protocol exploits**, necessitating robust security measures.

Cryptocurrency security involves **protecting digital assets, securing blockchain transactions, and preventing unauthorized access to wallets, exchanges, and DeFi platforms**. Threat actors target **private keys, decentralized applications (dApps), and smart contracts** to steal funds and manipulate blockchain ecosystems.

Understanding blockchain security principles is essential for **cryptocurrency investors, developers, cybersecurity professionals, and businesses leveraging blockchain-based solutions**.

11.2 Fundamentals of Blockchain Security

Blockchain is a **distributed ledger technology (DLT)** that records transactions in a **decentralized and tamper-resistant manner**. Each block contains a **cryptographic hash of the previous block**, forming an immutable chain.

11.2.1 Core Security Properties of Blockchain

1. **Decentralization:** No central authority controls the blockchain, reducing the risk of **single-point failures**.
2. **Immutability:** Once recorded, transactions cannot be **altered or deleted**, preventing data tampering.
3. **Cryptographic Security:** Transactions are secured using **asymmetric encryption and digital signatures**.
4. **Consensus Mechanisms:** Networks validate transactions using **Proof of Work (PoW), Proof of Stake (PoS), or hybrid consensus models**.

Example:

- The **Bitcoin blockchain** uses **PoW mining** to secure transactions, requiring computational effort to validate new blocks.

Despite its security advantages, blockchain technology is vulnerable to **smart contract bugs, cryptographic key theft, double-spending attacks, and Sybil attacks**.

11.3 Cryptocurrency Wallet Security

Cryptocurrency wallets store **private keys**, granting access to blockchain-based assets. Securing private keys is critical to **preventing theft, fraud, and unauthorized transactions**.

11.3.1 Types of Cryptocurrency Wallets

1. **Hot Wallets:** Connected to the internet, offering convenience but increasing hacking risks.

- **Examples:** MetaMask, Trust Wallet, Coinbase Wallet.

1. **Cold Wallets:** Offline storage providing **enhanced security** against online threats.

- **Examples:** Ledger Nano X, Trezor Model T.

1. **Paper Wallets:** Physical printouts of **private and public keys**, immune to online attacks but vulnerable to physical theft.
2. **Multi-Signature Wallets:** Require multiple private keys to authorize transactions, reducing the risk of **single-point compromises**.

11.3.2 Common Cryptocurrency Wallet Threats

- **Phishing Attacks:** Cybercriminals impersonate wallet providers to **steal private keys and recovery phrases**.
- **Malware and Keyloggers:** Malicious software records keystrokes to extract **private keys**.
- **Clipboard Hijacking:** Malware modifies copied wallet addresses, redirecting funds to attacker-controlled wallets.
- **Supply Chain Attacks:** Hardware wallet manufacturers may be **compromised**, distributing **preloaded malware**.

Best Practices for Wallet Security:

- Store private keys in **cold wallets or air-gapped devices**.
- Enable **multi-factor authentication (MFA) on exchange accounts**.
- Use **passphrase encryption** for wallet backups.
- Verify transactions before confirming wallet addresses.

11.4 Smart Contract Security and Common Vulnerabilities

Smart contracts are **self-executing code deployed on blockchain networks** to automate transactions and agreements. However, flaws in **smart contract logic** can lead to **exploits, asset theft, and financial losses**.

11.4.1 Common Smart Contract Vulnerabilities

1. **Reentrancy Attacks:** Exploits recursive function calls to drain contract funds before balance updates.
2. **Integer Overflows and Underflows:** Poor arithmetic handling allows **unexpected fund withdrawals**.
3. **Access Control Flaws:** Unauthorized users execute **restricted smart contract functions**.
4. **Denial-of-Service (DoS) Attacks:** Attackers spam transactions to **block contract execution**.
5. **Oracle Manipulation:** Attackers feed **manipulated price data** to blockchain oracles, influencing **DeFi transactions**.

Example:

- The **DAO Hack (2016)** exploited a **reentrancy vulnerability**, leading to the theft of **$60 million in Ethereum (ETH)**.

11.4.2 Best Practices for Smart Contract Security

- Conduct **formal verification and unit testing** before deploying contracts.
- Use **time-lock mechanisms** to prevent **instant fund withdrawals**.
- Implement **upgradable smart contract frameworks** to patch vulnerabilities.
- Engage in **third-party security audits** for contract verification.

11.5 Decentralized Finance (DeFi) Security Risks

Decentralized Finance (DeFi) platforms facilitate **peer-to-peer lending, yield farming, and automated trading** without intermediaries. However, DeFi protocols are frequent targets of **hacks, flash loan attacks, and price manipulation schemes**.

11.5.1 Common DeFi Security Threats

- **Flash Loan Exploits:** Attackers borrow **large amounts of crypto without collateral** to manipulate markets.
- **Rug Pull Scams:** Developers create **fake DeFi projects**, withdraw liquidity, and abandon platforms.
- **Impermanent Loss Attacks:** Manipulated trading activity drains liquidity from **automated market makers (AMMs)**.
- **Exploitative Liquidity Pool Draining:** Vulnerabilities in **smart contract pools** allow cybercriminals to withdraw funds.

Example:

- The **Poly Network hack (2021)** resulted in **$600 million in stolen funds**, making it one of the largest DeFi attacks in history.

11.5.2 DeFi Security Best Practices

- Use **multi-signature governance models** to prevent **unauthorized fund withdrawals**.
- Conduct **on-chain transaction monitoring** to detect suspicious activities.
- Implement **oracle price verification mechanisms** to prevent **price manipulation attacks**.
- Require **security audits for DeFi smart contracts** before launch.

11.6 Exchange Security and Cryptocurrency Fraud Prevention

Cryptocurrency exchanges are **prime targets** for hackers due to their role in **storing user funds and processing high-value transactions**.

11.6.1 Exchange Security Threats

- **Exchange Breaches:** Cybercriminals exploit **weak security controls** to steal digital assets.
- **Insider Threats:** Employees with privileged access **collaborate with hackers** to drain exchange reserves.
- **Pump-and-Dump Schemes:** Manipulated price movements **artificially inflate or crash asset values**.
- **SIM-Swapping Attacks:** Attackers take over mobile numbers to **bypass exchange authentication systems**.

Example:

- The **Mt. Gox breach (2014)** led to the **loss of 850,000 Bitcoin (BTC)** due to internal fraud and external cyber attacks.

11.6.2 Cryptocurrency Exchange Security Best Practices

- Use **cold storage solutions** to protect exchange reserves.
- Require **multi-signature authorization** for withdrawals.
- Implement **AI-based fraud detection** to identify suspicious transactions.
- Enforce **strict KYC (Know Your Customer) and AML (Anti-Money Laundering) compliance**.

11.7 Regulatory Compliance in Blockchain and Cryptocurrency Security

Cryptocurrency regulations vary globally, with governments enforcing **KYC, AML, and tax compliance policies** to prevent **illicit transactions**.

11.7.1 Global Cryptocurrency Regulations

Regulation	Jurisdiction	Key Compliance Requirements
Financial Action Task Force (FATF) Travel Rule	Global	Requires crypto exchanges to share sender and recipient transaction data.
U.S. Infrastructure Investment and Jobs Act (2021)	United States	Mandates crypto tax reporting for transactions over $10,000.
Markets in Crypto-Assets (MiCA)	European Union	Establishes legal standards for digital assets and stablecoins.
China's Crypto Ban (2021)	China	Prohibits all cryptocurrency transactions and mining activities.

11.7.2 Compliance Best Practices

- Implement **AI-driven transaction monitoring** to detect **suspicious crypto activities**.
- Ensure **KYC verification for all users on crypto platforms**.
- Adopt **blockchain forensics tools** to track illicit transactions.

Conclusion

Blockchain and cryptocurrency security require **robust encryption, private key protection, smart contract auditing, and DeFi risk mitigation strategies**. Organizations and investors must **implement security best practices, leverage blockchain forensics, and stay compliant with evolving cryptocurrency regulations** to mitigate risks.

In **Chapter 12: Artificial Intelligence and Cybersecurity**, we will explore how **AI enhances cybersecurity defenses, automates threat detection, and predicts cyber attacks** using **machine learning and deep learning algorithms**.

Chapter 12

ARTIFICIAL INTELLIGENCE AND CYBERSECURITY

12.1 Introduction to AI in Cybersecurity

Artificial intelligence (AI) is transforming **cyber defense, threat detection, and incident response** by automating security processes and analyzing vast amounts of threat data. Cybersecurity professionals leverage **machine learning (ML), deep learning (DL), and neural networks** to identify **patterns, detect anomalies, and predict cyber threats before they materialize**.

AI-driven cybersecurity solutions enhance **network monitoring, endpoint protection, fraud detection, and cyber threat intelligence** by processing real-time data and responding to cyber incidents with **minimal human intervention**. However, as AI strengthens security, **cybercriminals also use AI to enhance their attack methodologies, develop adaptive malware, and bypass traditional security defenses**.

This chapter explores the **role of AI in cybersecurity, its applications, advantages, and the risks associated with AI-powered cyber attacks**.

12.2 Machine Learning in Cybersecurity

Machine learning (ML) is a subset of AI that **enables security systems to learn from data patterns and improve detection capabilities without explicit programming**. ML models analyze **historical cyber attack data, identify**

anomalies, and detect malicious activities in real-time.

12.2.1 Supervised vs. Unsupervised Learning in Cybersecurity

Machine Learning Type	Function in Cybersecurity	Use Case Example
Supervised Learning	Trained on labeled datasets to recognize known attack patterns.	Detects known **malware signatures** and classifies spam emails.
Unsupervised Learning	Identifies unknown attack patterns without labeled datasets.	Detects **zero-day attacks and insider threats** through anomaly detection.
Reinforcement Learning	AI agents learn by making security decisions and improving over time.	Automates **intrusion prevention and adaptive network defense.**

12.2.2 Applications of Machine Learning in Cybersecurity

1. **Behavioral Analysis:** Detects abnormal user behavior that may indicate **insider threats or compromised accounts**.
2. **Malware Detection:** Identifies new malware strains by analyzing **code similarities and execution behaviors**.
3. **Network Intrusion Detection:** Flags **suspicious traffic patterns** that deviate from normal activity.
4. **Email Security and Phishing Prevention:** Classifies phishing emails by analyzing **email headers, content, and sender behavior**.

12.3 AI-Powered Threat Detection and Response

Traditional cybersecurity solutions rely on **static rules and signature-based detection**, which **struggle to detect unknown threats and rapidly evolving attack techniques**. AI-powered security systems utilize **adaptive learning and automation** to enhance **real-time threat detection and incident response**.

12.3.1 AI in Endpoint Security

- **Next-Generation Antivirus (NGAV):** Uses **machine learning algorithms** to detect and block **fileless malware, polymorphic viruses, and zero-day exploits**.
- **Endpoint Detection and Response (EDR):** Monitors **endpoint activity in real-time** to detect **advanced persistent threats (APTs)**.

12.3.2 AI in Network Security

- **AI-Driven Intrusion Detection Systems (IDS):** Identifies **unauthorized access attempts and unusual network behavior**.
- **Automated Threat Hunting:** Uses AI to analyze security logs, **detect lateral movement, and predict attacker strategies**.

12.3.3 AI in Cloud Security

- **Automated Cloud Security Posture Management (CSPM):** Identifies misconfigurations in **AWS, Azure, and Google Cloud environments**.
- **AI-Driven Identity and Access Management (IAM):** Uses behavior-based authentication to detect **compromised accounts**.

AI enhances **security efficiency, reduces response times, and minimizes human errors**, making it a **critical component of modern cybersecurity strategies**.

12.4 Adversarial AI: How Cybercriminals Use AI in Attacks

While AI strengthens cybersecurity defenses, **cybercriminals also exploit AI to enhance attack methodologies**. Adversarial AI refers to **malicious uses of artificial intelligence** to develop **evasive malware, conduct automated phishing campaigns, and bypass security controls**.

12.4.1 AI-Driven Cyber Attacks

- **Deepfake-Based Social Engineering:** Attackers use **AI-generated deepfake voices and videos** to impersonate executives and conduct financial fraud.
- **AI-Powered Malware:** Adaptive malware evolves to **evade traditional antivirus detection**.
- **Automated Phishing Attacks:** AI analyzes social media and corporate emails to generate **highly personalized phishing campaigns**.
- **AI-Powered Credential Stuffing:** Automated bots test stolen credentials on multiple platforms to gain unauthorized access.

Example:

- In 2019, cybercriminals used an **AI-powered voice deepfake** to impersonate a CEO and successfully **scammed a company out of $243,000** through a fraudulent wire transfer.

12.4.2 Defending Against AI-Powered Threats

- Implement **AI-based fraud detection** to identify **deepfake impersonation attacks**.
- Use **behavioral biometrics** to detect **anomalies in login patterns and access requests**.
- Deploy **adversarial machine learning techniques** to train security models against AI-driven attacks.

Organizations must **continuously evolve their cybersecurity strategies to counter AI-enhanced cyber threats**.

12.5 AI and Automation in Cyber Threat Intelligence

Cyber threat intelligence (CTI) relies on **AI-driven data analysis** to identify **threat actors, attack trends, and emerging vulnerabilities**.

12.5.1 AI in Threat Intelligence Gathering

1. **Dark Web Monitoring:** AI scans darknet marketplaces for **leaked credentials and cybercriminal activities**.
2. **Malware Classification:** Machine learning categorizes malware into **families based on code similarities**.
3. **Threat Attribution:** AI maps cyber attacks to **known threat actors and nation-state cyber units**.

12.5.2 AI in Security Automation and Incident Response

1. **Security Orchestration, Automation, and Response (SOAR):**

- Automates **threat detection, investigation, and remediation**.
- Reduces **incident response times by automating security workflows**.

1. **Predictive Threat Analytics:**

- AI models forecast **potential attack patterns** based on historical data.
- Enhances **proactive defense strategies** by predicting **high-risk attack vectors**.

AI enhances **cyber threat intelligence by processing vast amounts of data, identifying emerging attack trends, and automating threat response actions**.

12.6 Ethical and Legal Challenges of AI in Cybersecurity

AI-driven cybersecurity presents **ethical, legal, and regulatory challenges** related to **data privacy, bias in AI decision-making, and adversarial AI risks.**

12.6.1 Ethical Challenges of AI in Cybersecurity

- **AI Bias in Security Decision-Making:**Machine learning models may exhibit **biases that lead to false positives or missed threats.**
- **Privacy Concerns in AI-Driven Surveillance:**AI-powered security systems **analyze vast amounts of personal data**, raising **privacy and ethical concerns.**
- **AI Arms Race in Cyber Warfare:**Nation-state actors invest in **AI-powered cyber weapons**, escalating **global cyber conflicts.**

12.6.2 Legal and Compliance Challenges

- **AI in GDPR and Data Privacy Regulations:**AI-driven security solutions must comply with **data protection laws and privacy regulations.**
- **AI Liability in Automated Cybersecurity Decisions:**Organizations must define **legal responsibilities for AI-driven security actions and false positives.**

Organizations must implement **ethical AI governance frameworks** to ensure that **AI-powered cybersecurity remains compliant with legal and ethical standards.**

Conclusion

Artificial intelligence is **revolutionizing cybersecurity** by enabling **real-time threat detection, automated incident response, and predictive analytics.** However, as AI strengthens defenses, **cybercriminals also use AI to enhance attack methodologies, requiring organizations to adopt AI-driven threat** intelligence and security automation.

In **Chapter 13: Quantum Computing and the Future of Cybersecurity**, we will explore **the impact of quantum computing on cryptography, emerging quantum threats, and the development of quantum-resistant security measures**.

Chapter 13

QUANTUM COMPUTING AND THE FUTURE OF CYBERSECURITY

13.1 Introduction to Quantum Computing and Cybersecurity

Quantum computing represents **a paradigm shift in computational power**, leveraging **quantum mechanics to perform calculations at speeds unattainable by classical computers**. While quantum technology promises breakthroughs in **scientific research, cryptography, artificial intelligence, and material sciences**, it also presents **significant threats to modern cybersecurity systems**.

Current encryption standards rely on **mathematical complexity** to secure data, making brute-force decryption infeasible with classical computing. However, quantum computers possess the potential to **break widely used encryption algorithms, undermine cryptographic security, and expose sensitive data**.

Cybersecurity professionals, governments, and enterprises must prepare for **the advent of quantum computing by transitioning to quantum-resistant cryptographic systems and implementing quantum-safe security frameworks**.

13.2 How Quantum Computing Works

Quantum computing is based on **quantum bits (qubits)**, which differ from classical binary bits in their ability to exist in **multiple states simultaneously**. This unique property allows quantum computers to perform **parallel computations** and solve complex problems at an **exponentially faster rate** than traditional computers.

13.2.1 Key Principles of Quantum Computing

1. **Superposition:**

- Unlike classical bits (0 or 1), **qubits can exist in multiple states simultaneously**.
- This enables quantum computers to **process vast amounts of information at once**.

1. **Entanglement:**

- Quantum particles become **interconnected**, meaning that the state of one qubit instantly affects the state of another, even at great distances.
- This property allows for **ultra-secure quantum communication channels**.

1. **Quantum Interference:**

- Quantum computers use **wave interference to optimize computational pathways**, increasing efficiency.

13.2.2 Advantages of Quantum Computing in Cybersecurity

- **Ultra-Secure Communications:**Quantum Key Distribution (QKD) enables **unbreakable encryption** using quantum entanglement.
- **Faster Threat Detection:**Quantum computing accelerates **cyber threat intelligence and real-time anomaly detection**.
- **Enhanced Cryptographic Hashing:**Quantum algorithms can generate **collision-resistant hash functions**, improving digital forensics and blockchain security.

Despite these advantages, quantum computing also poses **severe risks** to current cryptographic security models.

13.3 The Quantum Threat to Cryptography

Modern cybersecurity depends on **asymmetric encryption**, which relies on **factorization, discrete logarithms, and elliptic curve mathematics** to secure data. Quantum computing **threatens these encryption standards** by solving complex mathematical problems exponentially faster than classical computers.

13.3.1 Shor's Algorithm and Breaking Public-Key Cryptography

- **Shor's Algorithm** is a quantum algorithm capable of **factoring large prime numbers exponentially faster** than classical methods.
- This renders widely used encryption schemes such as **RSA, Diffie-Hellman, and Elliptic Curve Cryptography (ECC) obsolete**.

Example Impact:

- **RSA-2048 encryption**, currently unbreakable with classical computers, could be **decrypted in minutes** with a sufficiently powerful quantum computer.

13.3.2 Grover's Algorithm and Symmetric Key Encryption

- **Grover's Algorithm** reduces the time needed to brute-force **symmetric encryption keys**.
- It weakens ciphers like **AES-256**, forcing organizations to **double key sizes to maintain security**.

13.3.3 Blockchain and Cryptocurrency Vulnerabilities

- Quantum computing threatens **blockchain immutability by reversing cryptographic hashes**.
- Quantum attacks could break **Bitcoin's ECDSA (Elliptic Curve Digital Signature Algorithm)**, allowing attackers to **forge transactions and steal funds**.

Example Risk:

- A sufficiently advanced quantum computer could **generate private keys from public addresses**, compromising **entire cryptocurrency networks**.

These risks necessitate the **urgent development of quantum-resistant cryptographic solutions** to maintain digital security.

13.4 Post-Quantum Cryptography (PQC) and Quantum-Safe Security

To mitigate quantum threats, cryptographers are developing **post-quantum cryptography (PQC)**—encryption algorithms that remain secure against quantum attacks.

13.4.1 Post-Quantum Cryptographic Algorithms

- **Lattice-Based Cryptography:**Uses **multidimensional lattice structures** that quantum computers struggle to solve.
- Algorithms: **NTRU, CRYSTALS-Kyber, CRYSTALS-Dilithium.**
- **Multivariate Polynomial Cryptography:**Relies on **non-linear polynomial equations** for security.
- Algorithm: **Rainbow.**
- **Hash-Based Cryptography:**Utilizes **hash trees (Merkle signatures) for post-quantum digital signatures.**
- Algorithm: **SPHINCS+.**
- **Code-Based Cryptography:**Uses **error-correcting codes** for encryption.
- Algorithm: **McEliece.**

13.4.2 Quantum-Safe Encryption Strategies

- **Hybrid Cryptographic Models:** Combines **classic encryption** with **quantum-resistant algorithms**.
- **Quantum Key Distribution (QKD):** Uses quantum entanglement for **unbreakable encryption keys**.
- **Longer Key Sizes:** Increases **AES key lengths to mitigate Grover's Algorithm attacks**.

Organizations must **prepare for post-quantum security now**, as the transition to quantum-resistant cryptographic infrastructure requires significant **technological upgrades and regulatory compliance efforts**.

13.5 Quantum Computing in Cyber Defense and Threat Intelligence

While quantum computing threatens **modern encryption**, it also enhances cybersecurity **defense mechanisms, real-time analytics, and predictive threat intelligence**.

13.5.1 Quantum-Enhanced Cybersecurity Applications

1. **Quantum Cryptography for Ultra-Secure Networks:**

- Quantum communication systems use **QKD (Quantum Key Distribution)** to prevent data interception.
- Nations are developing **quantum-secure communication grids** for military and financial networks.

1. **Quantum-Based Threat Detection:**

- Quantum AI improves **real-time cyber threat hunting and malware analysis**.
- Speeds up **pattern recognition in cyber threat intelligence**.

1. **Quantum-Resistant Blockchain Protocols:**

- Researchers are designing **quantum-safe blockchain algorithms** resistant to cryptographic attacks.
- Future cryptocurrencies may integrate **lattice-based cryptographic signatures**.

13.5.2 Nations Advancing Quantum Cybersecurity

- **China's Quantum Satellite (Micius):** Demonstrated the first **quantum-encrypted global communication system**.
- **U.S. National Quantum Initiative (NQI):** Invests in **quantum-resistant cryptographic research**.
- **European Union's Quantum Flagship Program:** Develops **post-quantum encryption standards**.

Quantum computing will **redefine cybersecurity**, requiring global organizations to **adopt quantum-secure encryption and develop AI-powered defense mechanisms**.

13.6 Preparing for the Quantum Era: Next Steps in Cybersecurity

13.6.1 Steps Organizations Must Take

- **Assess Quantum Readiness:**Conduct **quantum risk assessments** to identify encryption vulnerabilities.
- **Upgrade to Post-Quantum Cryptography:**Implement **NIST-approved post-quantum cryptographic algorithms**.
- **Adopt Hybrid Encryption Strategies:**Combine **classical and quantum-resistant encryption models** during the transition phase.
- **Deploy Quantum-Secure Communication Systems:**Integrate **Quantum Key Distribution (QKD)** into critical infrastructure networks.
- **Train Cybersecurity Teams in Quantum Security:**Educate professionals on **post-quantum encryption and quantum cyber threats**.

Organizations that **proactively transition to quantum-safe security architectures** will **mitigate risks and maintain resilience** as quantum computing advances.

Conclusion

Quantum computing introduces both **groundbreaking opportunities and significant cybersecurity threats**. While **classical encryption methods face obsolescence, post-quantum cryptography and quantum-resistant security measures will ensure continued protection**. Governments, enterprises, and security researchers must **prepare for the quantum shift by integrating quantum-safe encryption and AI-driven defense mechanisms**.

In **Chapter 14: Cybersecurity in the Age of the Metaverse**, we will explore **the security challenges of virtual worlds, decentralized identities, and digital asset protection in the evolving metaverse landscape**.

Chapter 14

CYBERSECURITY IN THE AGE OF THE METAVERSE

14.1 Introduction to Metaverse Security

The metaverse is an emerging **digital ecosystem that integrates virtual reality (VR), augmented reality (AR), decentralized finance (DeFi), non-fungible tokens (NFTs), and blockchain-based identities**. It enables users to **engage in virtual economies, attend digital events, interact in 3D spaces, and own virtual assets**.

However, the metaverse also introduces **new cybersecurity risks, privacy concerns, digital identity theft, and financial fraud**. Cybercriminals exploit vulnerabilities in **smart contracts, digital identities, virtual asset ownership, and decentralized authentication systems** to carry out large-scale cyber attacks.

Organizations, developers, and users must implement **robust security frameworks, decentralized identity management, and blockchain-based access control** to protect metaverse environments from **hacking, fraud, and unauthorized exploitation**.

14.2 Cyber Threats in the Metaverse

14.2.1 Identity Theft and Digital Impersonation

- **Metaverse identity theft** occurs when attackers hijack **decentralized digital IDs, NFT avatars, or blockchain-based credentials.**
- **Deepfake AI-driven avatars** allow cybercriminals to impersonate real users.

Example:

- Hackers use **stolen NFT avatars and VR profiles** to gain unauthorized access to **metaverse financial accounts and property.**

14.2.2 Smart Contract Exploits in Virtual Economies

- Smart contracts facilitate **metaverse transactions, digital asset ownership, and decentralized payments.**
- Vulnerabilities in smart contract code lead to **rug pulls, flash loan exploits, and unauthorized withdrawals.**

Example:

- **Axie Infinity's Ronin Bridge hack (2022)** resulted in the theft of **$620 million in cryptocurrency from metaverse-based transactions.**

14.2.3 Phishing and Social Engineering Attacks

- Cybercriminals exploit metaverse **social interactions** to conduct **phishing scams, credential theft, and impersonation fraud.**
- Fake metaverse applications trick users into **revealing private keys and login credentials.**

Example:

- Attackers create **fraudulent VR-based investment platforms** to steal **DeFi assets and cryptocurrency holdings**.

14.2.4 Virtual Property Hijacking

- Attackers take control of **NFT-based land, metaverse businesses, and tokenized assets**.
- Weak authentication mechanisms allow unauthorized transfers of **digital real estate and virtual collectibles**.

Example:

- A hacker exploits **blockchain smart contract vulnerabilities** to seize ownership of **tokenized metaverse properties**.

14.2.5 Privacy Breaches and Data Exploitation

- **VR headsets, AR applications, and AI-driven avatars** collect **massive amounts of biometric and behavioral data**.
- Cybercriminals can extract **facial recognition data, motion tracking patterns, and real-time speech analysis**.

Example:

- An attacker hijacks a **VR chat session to eavesdrop on private business negotiations in a metaverse corporate meeting**.

Cybersecurity professionals must implement **strong encryption, decentralized authentication, and AI-driven fraud detection** to secure metaverse environments.

14.3 Decentralized Identity (DID) and Blockchain-Based Authentication

Traditional authentication methods **rely on centralized servers**, making them vulnerable to **hacks, data breaches, and identity theft**. The metaverse requires **decentralized identity (DID) frameworks** and blockchain-based authentication to ensure secure access.

14.3.1 How Decentralized Identity Works

- Users control their **digital identity credentials through blockchain wallets**.
- Digital identity is stored on **decentralized ledgers**, reducing reliance on **centralized identity providers**.
- Users verify transactions using **biometric authentication and cryptographic signatures**.

14.3.2 Blockchain-Based Authentication Mechanisms

- **Self-Sovereign Identity (SSI):** Users manage **metaverse identities** without relying on a central authority.
- **Zero-Knowledge Proofs (ZKPs):** Users prove identity attributes without revealing sensitive data.
- **Multi-Signature Wallets:** Secure access to **metaverse assets using multiple authentication factors**.

Example:

- A metaverse marketplace uses **DID-based logins instead of traditional usernames and passwords**, preventing credential theft.

Organizations must integrate **blockchain-based identity verification** to prevent **identity fraud, account takeovers, and digital asset theft**.

14.4 Smart Contract Security and DeFi Protection in the Metaverse

The metaverse relies on **smart contracts for financial transactions, NFT ownership, and decentralized exchanges (DEXs)**. However, **poorly coded smart contracts introduce severe security vulnerabilities**.

14.4.1 Common Smart Contract Vulnerabilities in the Metaverse

- **Reentrancy Attacks:** Exploit recursive function calls to **drain smart contract balances**.
- **Oracle Manipulation:** Attackers feed **false market data** to influence metaverse asset prices.
- **Access Control Weaknesses:** Unauthorized users gain **control of smart contract-based assets**.

14.4.2 Securing Smart Contracts in Metaverse Transactions

- Conduct **third-party audits** of smart contract code before deployment.
- Use **multi-signature approvals** for high-value metaverse asset transfers.
- Implement **circuit breakers** to pause compromised smart contracts.

Example:

- A metaverse-based **real estate NFT platform integrates AI-driven smart contract analysis to detect vulnerabilities before deployment**.

Organizations must ensure **continuous security monitoring of DeFi smart contracts** to prevent metaverse financial fraud.

14.5 Virtual Reality (VR) and Augmented Reality (AR) Security Risks

Metaverse environments utilize **VR and AR technologies**, which introduce **new attack vectors for hackers**.

14.5.1 VR and AR Cybersecurity Threats

- **Man-in-the-Middle (MITM) Attacks:** Hackers intercept **VR-based communications and financial transactions**.
- **Biometric Data Exploitation:** AI-driven deepfake avatars **mimic real users, bypassing facial recognition security**.
- **Virtual Espionage:** Attackers infiltrate **private VR spaces to gather confidential intelligence**.

14.5.2 Strengthening VR and AR Security

- **End-to-End Encryption (E2EE):** Protects **VR-based voice, chat, and transaction data**.
- **Biometric Spoofing Detection:** Prevents **AI-generated identity impersonation**.
- **Encrypted Data Transmission in AR Overlays:** Secures **AR-based real-time data feeds**.

Example:

- A corporate metaverse conference enforces **biometric authentication and E2EE for secure business meetings**.

Cybersecurity professionals must **develop AI-driven anomaly detection and identity verification systems** to secure **VR and AR environments**.

14.6 Regulatory Compliance and Governance in the Metaverse

The metaverse presents **legal and regulatory challenges** due to its decentralized nature. Governments and enterprises must establish **global cybersecurity policies for digital identity, asset protection, and fraud prevention**.

14.6.1 Key Metaverse Cybersecurity Regulations

Regulation	Jurisdiction	Focus Area
GDPR (General Data Protection Regulation)	European Union	Protects biometric data and user privacy in VR environments.
CCPA (California Consumer Privacy Act)	United States	Regulates collection of user data in metaverse applications.
MiCA (Markets in Crypto-Assets Regulation)	European Union	Ensures compliance for metaverse-based financial transactions.
SEC Crypto Regulations	United States	Oversees DeFi platforms and NFT financial activities.

14.6.2 Compliance Strategies for Metaverse Security

- Implement **GDPR-compliant biometric data protection** for metaverse platforms.
- Enforce **AML (Anti-Money Laundering) measures** for DeFi transactions.
- Require **blockchain-based transparency** for NFT ownership records.

Example:

- A global metaverse gaming platform **integrates regulatory-compliant identity verification for financial transactions**.

Regulatory bodies must **adapt legal frameworks to address the cybersecurity**

risks of decentralized metaverse ecosystems.

Conclusion

Cybersecurity in the metaverse requires **a multi-layered defense strategy combining blockchain authentication, AI-driven fraud detection, VR security enhancements, and smart contract auditing**. As the metaverse evolves, organizations must **proactively implement decentralized identity management, quantum-resistant encryption, and global cybersecurity compliance frameworks** to protect users from **identity theft, digital fraud, and virtual asset hijacking**.

In **Chapter 15: The Future of Cybersecurity and Emerging Threats**, we will explore **next-generation cyber threats, AI-enhanced cyber warfare, and the evolution of global cybersecurity strategies**.

Chapter 15

THE FUTURE OF CYBERSECURITY AND EMERGING THREATS

15.1 Introduction to the Future of Cybersecurity

The **evolution of cyber threats, digital warfare, and artificial intelligence-driven attacks** is reshaping the cybersecurity landscape. As **technology advances**, cybercriminals adopt **more sophisticated tactics**, leveraging **automation, deepfake AI, quantum computing, and advanced persistent threats (APTs)** to breach even the most secure infrastructures.

Cybersecurity professionals must prepare for **the next generation of cyber threats**, integrating **zero-trust architectures, AI-driven security models, post-quantum encryption, and global threat intelligence sharing** to mitigate risks. This chapter explores **emerging cybersecurity threats, the impact of AI-driven cyber warfare, and future defense strategies** that will define the **next era of digital security**.

15.2 Emerging Cybersecurity Threats

The **rapid expansion of cloud computing, 5G networks, the Internet of Things (IoT), and decentralized finance (DeFi)** presents **new attack vectors** for cybercriminals.

15.2.1 AI-Powered Cyber Attacks

- **AI-Driven Malware:** Adaptive malware **evolves in real-time**, evading traditional antivirus detection.
- **Deepfake Identity Fraud:** AI-generated deepfake **videos and voice manipulations** trick organizations into **unauthorized transactions**.
- **Automated Phishing Attacks:** Machine learning enhances phishing emails, making them **indistinguishable from legitimate messages**.

Example:

- Cybercriminals used **AI-powered voice deepfakes** to impersonate a CEO, resulting in a **fraudulent $35 million bank transfer**.

15.2.2 Quantum-Enabled Cyber Warfare

- **Shor's Algorithm** will break **RSA and ECC encryption**, making **current cryptographic standards obsolete**.
- **Nation-state quantum programs** will develop **unbreakable encryption for classified government communications**.

Example:

- A quantum computer could decrypt **classified intelligence archives**, exposing sensitive government and military operations.

15.2.3 Cyber Threats in 5G Networks and IoT Devices

- **Unpatched IoT devices** provide hackers with **entry points into corporate and smart home networks**.
- **5G-enabled botnets** amplify **distributed denial-of-service (DDoS) attacks** at an unprecedented scale.

Example:

- The **Mirai botnet attack** exploited **unsecured IoT devices,** taking down major **internet infrastructure providers.**

15.2.4 Cyber Warfare and Nation-State Attacks

- **AI-generated cyber weapons** autonomously detect and exploit **vulnerabilities in critical infrastructure.**
- **State-sponsored cyber attacks** target **power grids, defense networks, and financial institutions.**

Example:

- The **NotPetya cyber attack (2017)** was attributed to **Russian military intelligence,** causing **$10 billion in global damages.**

The **rise of AI-enhanced cyber warfare, quantum hacking, and IoT vulnerabilities** necessitates **advanced cybersecurity strategies to defend against next-generation cyber threats.**

15.3 The Evolution of Cyber Warfare

Cyber warfare has escalated from **basic denial-of-service attacks to sophisticated AI-driven digital conflicts** between nation-states. Governments are developing **cyber weapons capable of disrupting economies, military operations, and national security.**

15.3.1 Cyber Warfare Tactics

1. **AI-Assisted Espionage:** AI analyzes **global internet traffic and military communications** for intelligence gathering.
2. **Cyber-Sabotage of Critical Infrastructure:** Attacks target **power grids,**

nuclear facilities, and transportation systems.

3. **AI-Generated Misinformation Campaigns:** Deepfake videos manipulate **elections, stock markets, and public opinion**.

4. **Autonomous Cyber Weapons:** AI-powered malware **self-replicates, adapts, and spreads across global networks**.

Example:

- China and Russia have **state-sponsored cyber units** dedicated to conducting **AI-driven cyber warfare and economic sabotage**.

15.3.2 Defending Against Cyber Warfare

- Governments must **implement quantum-safe encryption and AI-powered intrusion detection systems**.
- **Cyber defense treaties** will be necessary to prevent **AI-driven cyber conflicts** between global superpowers.

Cyber warfare is shifting toward **autonomous, AI-driven attack methodologies**, requiring **advanced cyber defense infrastructures** to mitigate **global digital conflicts**.

15.4 AI-Driven Cybersecurity Defense Mechanisms

As **AI-powered cyber threats increase**, organizations must integrate **machine learning-driven defense strategies** to **automate threat detection, real-time response, and predictive analytics**.

15.4.1 AI in Next-Generation Cybersecurity

- **Self-Healing Networks:** AI-driven security frameworks detect **intrusions and autonomously repair system vulnerabilities**.
- **Automated Incident Response (AIR):** Machine learning **isolates infected**

systems and deploys **countermeasures** in real-time.
- **AI-Powered Cyber Threat Intelligence:** AI scans **dark web markets and cybercriminal networks** to predict emerging threats.

15.4.2 AI-Enhanced Behavioral Analytics

- **Deep learning algorithms** detect **anomalies in financial transactions, login attempts, and biometric authentication**.
- **Neural networks** analyze **social engineering patterns**, preventing **real-time phishing attacks**.

Example:

- **Google's AI-driven fraud detection system** identifies and blocks **sophisticated cyber fraud attacks** before execution.

15.4.3 AI and Blockchain Integration for Cybersecurity

- **Decentralized AI models** protect **data integrity by combining blockchain's immutability with AI's anomaly detection**.
- **AI-powered blockchain auditing** prevents **smart contract exploits and DeFi fraud**.

Organizations must **integrate AI-driven cybersecurity frameworks** to combat **automated cyber threats and adversarial AI attacks**.

15.5 The Future of Cybersecurity Frameworks and Global Regulations

Cybersecurity laws and regulations will evolve to **address the challenges of AI-driven cybercrime, digital identity security, and blockchain-based fraud prevention**.

15.5.1 The Expansion of Cybersecurity Regulations

- **AI Cybercrime Laws:** Governments will **criminalize AI-powered hacking, deepfake fraud, and autonomous cyber attacks**.
- **Quantum Cryptography Compliance:** Organizations will be **required to transition to quantum-resistant encryption**.
- **Global Cyber Defense Alliances:** Nations will establish **international treaties to prevent AI-driven cyber warfare**.

15.5.2 Strengthening Cybersecurity Resilience

- **Zero-Trust Security Architecture:** Organizations will implement **continuous identity verification and AI-powered access control**.
- **Cyber Resilience Frameworks:** Enterprises will integrate **self-repairing, AI-driven security infrastructures**.
- **Cyber Insurance Expansion:** Insurers will require **AI-based threat monitoring for cybersecurity coverage eligibility**.

15.5.3 Future Cybersecurity Job Market and Skills Demand

- **AI-Powered Security Analysts:** Professionals specializing in **machine learning-based cybersecurity** will be in **high demand**.
- **Quantum Cryptography Specialists:** Experts in **post-quantum encryption and cryptanalysis** will be essential.
- **Cyber Warfare Defense Engineers:** Organizations will require **specialists in AI-driven cyber defense and digital warfare countermeasures**.

Cybersecurity will evolve into **AI-driven, quantum-resistant, and decentralized security models**, requiring **global cooperation, legislative advancements, and advanced security intelligence networks**.

Conclusion

The future of cybersecurity will be defined by **AI-driven defense strategies, post-quantum cryptographic infrastructures, and automated cyber warfare countermeasures**. Organizations, governments, and cybersecurity professionals must **stay ahead of emerging threats by integrating AI, blockchain security, and real-time cyber resilience frameworks**.

In **Chapter 16: Building a Career in Cybersecurity**, we will explore **how professionals can develop expertise in AI cybersecurity, quantum cryptography, ethical hacking, and cyber warfare defense**, positioning themselves at the forefront of **next-generation cybersecurity careers**.

Chapter 16

BUILDING A CAREER IN CYBERSECURITY

16.1 Introduction to Cybersecurity Careers

Cybersecurity is one of the **fastest-growing fields**, offering lucrative opportunities in **ethical hacking, cyber defense, digital forensics, and threat
intelligence**. As **cybercrime evolves**, organizations require **highly skilled
security professionals** to **protect critical infrastructure, mitigate cyber risks,
and counteract sophisticated cyber threats**.

A career in cybersecurity requires **technical expertise, problem-solving
skills, continuous learning, and ethical responsibility**. This chapter provides
a **step-by-step guide to entering, advancing, and excelling in the cybersecurity industry**, covering **certifications, job roles, skills development, and
career pathways**.

16.2 Cybersecurity Career Pathways and Specializations

Cybersecurity offers **diverse career paths**, allowing professionals to specialize
in **offensive security, defensive operations, risk management, and cyber
intelligence**.

16.2.1 Offensive Cybersecurity Careers (Red Teaming and Ethical Hacking)

Red team professionals specialize in **simulating cyber attacks to test an organization's defenses**.
  Key Job Roles:

- **Ethical Hacker (Penetration Tester):** Simulates **real-world cyber attacks** to identify vulnerabilities.
- **Red Team Operator:** Conducts **advanced cyber adversary simulations**.
- **Exploit Developer:** Creates **custom hacking tools and zero-day exploits**.

Recommended Certifications:

- Certified Ethical Hacker (CEH)
- Offensive Security Certified Professional (OSCP)
- GIAC Penetration Tester (GPEN)

16.2.2 Defensive Cybersecurity Careers (Blue Teaming and SOC Operations)

Blue team professionals **detect, prevent, and respond to cyber threats** in real-time.
  Key Job Roles:

- **SOC Analyst (Security Operations Center):** Monitors **intrusion detection systems** and responds to incidents.
- **Incident Responder:** Investigates **cyber attacks and mitigates security breaches**.
- **Threat Intelligence Analyst:** Tracks **cybercriminal groups and nation-state threat actors**.

Recommended Certifications:

- Certified Information Systems Security Professional (CISSP)
- GIAC Certified Incident Handler (GCIH)
- CompTIA Cybersecurity Analyst (CySA+)

16.2.3 Cybersecurity Engineering and Architecture

Cybersecurity engineers **design, implement, and manage security infras-tructures**.
   Key Job Roles:

- **Security Engineer:** Builds **firewalls, intrusion prevention systems (IPS), and endpoint protection solutions**.
- **Cloud Security Engineer:** Secures **AWS, Azure, and Google Cloud environments**.
- **Cybersecurity Architect:** Develops **enterprise-wide security policies and frameworks**.

Recommended Certifications:

- Certified Cloud Security Professional (CCSP)
- GIAC Security Expert (GSE)
- AWS Certified Security – Specialty

16.2.4 Digital Forensics and Malware Analysis

Digital forensics specialists **investigate cybercrime, analyze malware, and recover compromised data**.
   Key Job Roles:

- **Digital Forensics Investigator:** Collects and analyzes **digital evidence for law enforcement and private firms**.
- **Malware Analyst:** Reverse-engineers **malicious software to develop detection signatures**.

- **Cybercrime Investigator:** Tracks **hackers, fraudsters, and insider threats**.

Recommended Certifications:

- GIAC Certified Forensic Analyst (GCFA)
- Certified Computer Examiner (CCE)
- CHFI (Computer Hacking Forensic Investigator)

16.2.5 Cyber Risk and Compliance

Cyber risk specialists **ensure organizations meet legal and regulatory security requirements**.
   Key Job Roles:

- **Compliance Analyst:** Ensures **adherence to cybersecurity regulations (GDPR, HIPAA, PCI-DSS)**.
- **Risk Manager:** Identifies and mitigates **cybersecurity risks affecting business operations**.
- **Security Auditor:** Conducts **penetration tests and security audits** for compliance verification.

Recommended Certifications:

- Certified Information Security Manager (CISM)
- Certified Information Systems Auditor (CISA)
- NIST Cybersecurity Framework (NCSF)

Cybersecurity professionals can specialize in **one or multiple career paths**, depending on their **interests, skill set, and long-term career goals**.

16.3 Technical Skills Required for Cybersecurity Careers

Cybersecurity professionals must develop **strong technical expertise** in **network security, cryptography, ethical hacking, and secure software development**.

16.3.1 Essential Technical Skills

Skill	Application in Cybersecurity
Networking and Protocols	Understanding TCP/IP, DNS, HTTP, VPNs, and firewalls.
Linux and Windows Security	Securing operating systems against malware and unauthorized access.
Programming and Scripting	Writing Python, Bash, and PowerShell scripts for security automation.
Penetration Testing	Identifying and exploiting vulnerabilities in web applications and networks.
Cryptography	Implementing encryption algorithms and secure key management.
Reverse Engineering	Analyzing malware and exploit code to develop countermeasures.

16.3.2 Soft Skills for Cybersecurity Professionals

Problem-Solving: Quickly analyzing **security incidents and developing effective countermeasures**.

Attention to Detail: Identifying **small anomalies in logs and attack patterns**.

Communication Skills: Explaining **complex security concepts to non-technical stakeholders**.

Cybersecurity professionals must **continuously improve both technical and analytical skills** to stay ahead of **evolving cyber threats**.

16.4 How to Get Started in Cybersecurity

Beginners can **enter the cybersecurity field** by following a structured approach to **skills development, certifications, and hands-on experience**.

16.4.1 Step-by-Step Guide to Starting a Cybersecurity Career

Learn Networking and Security Fundamentals

Study **TCP/IP, VPNs, firewalls, and intrusion detection systems**.

Take free courses on **CompTIA Security+ and Cisco Networking**.

Gain Hands-On Experience

Set up a **home lab using Kali Linux, Metasploit, and Wireshark**.

Participate in **Capture The Flag (CTF) competitions** to improve hacking skills.

Earn Entry-Level Certifications

Start with **CompTIA Security+, Cisco CyberOps, or GIAC GSEC**.

Apply for Entry-Level Cybersecurity Jobs

Look for roles such as **SOC Analyst, IT Security Administrator, or Junior Penetration Tester**.

Contribute to **open-source security projects** to build experience.

Develop Specialization in a Cybersecurity Niche

Advance into **ethical hacking, digital forensics, or cloud security**.

Earn advanced certifications like **OSCP, CISSP, or CCSP**.

Build a Professional Network

Join **cybersecurity communities, attend DEFCON and Black Hat conferences**.

Connect with cybersecurity professionals on **LinkedIn and GitHub**.

Continue Learning and Stay Updated

Cyber threats evolve rapidly; continuous learning is essential.

Follow **cybersecurity blogs, research papers, and vulnerability reports**.

Following this roadmap enables individuals to **transition into cybersecurity and secure high-paying job opportunities**.

16.5 Cybersecurity Salary Expectations and Career Growth

Cybersecurity professionals are **in high demand**, with salaries varying by **experience, specialization, and geographic location**.

16.5.1 Average Cybersecurity Salaries

Job Role	Average Salary (USD)
Entry-Level SOC Analyst	$65,000 - $85,000
Ethical Hacker / Penetration Tester	$90,000 - $140,000
Cybersecurity Engineer	$110,000 - $160,000
Chief Information Security Officer (CISO)	$200,000 - $500,000

Cybersecurity careers offer **long-term stability, high earning potential, and opportunities for career advancement**.

Conclusion

Building a career in cybersecurity requires **technical expertise, certifications, practical experience, and continuous learning**. With cyber threats becoming more sophisticated, **organizations seek highly skilled professionals to defend against cyber attacks and secure critical infrastructure**.

In **Chapter 17: Ethical Hacking and Cybersecurity Ethics**, we will explore **the responsibilities of ethical hackers, the legality of penetration testing, and the moral dilemmas in cybersecurity**.

Chapter 17

ETHICAL HACKING AND CYBERSECURITY ETHICS

17.1 Introduction to Ethical Hacking

Ethical hacking involves **identifying, exploiting, and mitigating vulnerabilities in computer systems, networks, and applications** with **legal authorization**. Ethical hackers, also known as **penetration testers or white-hat hackers**, use the same techniques as cybercriminals but with the objective of **strengthening security rather than causing harm**.

Ethical hacking is an essential component of **cyber defense strategies**, helping organizations **test their security infrastructure, assess risks, and prevent real-world cyber attacks**. However, **ethical and legal boundaries** must always be maintained, ensuring that security testing **adheres to cybersecurity laws, corporate policies, and industry regulations**.

This chapter explores **ethical hacking methodologies, legal considerations, industry best practices, and the moral responsibilities of cybersecurity professionals**.

17.2 Ethical Hacking vs. Malicious Hacking

There is a critical distinction between **ethical hackers, black-hat hackers, and gray-hat hackers**.

17.2.1 Categories of Hackers

Hacker Type	Characteristics	Intent
White-Hat Hackers (Ethical Hackers)	Conduct **authorized security assessments** to strengthen systems.	Improve security and **protect organizations.**
Black-Hat Hackers (Criminal Hackers)	Exploit vulnerabilities **illegally** for financial gain, espionage, or disruption.	Cause harm, steal data, and conduct cybercrime.
Gray-Hat Hackers	Identify security flaws **without permission** but may disclose findings.	Sometimes report vulnerabilities, but often operate in **legal gray areas.**

Ethical hackers must **operate strictly within legal guidelines**, ensuring that all security assessments are **approved by system owners and follow cybersecurity regulations**.

17.3 The Five Phases of Ethical Hacking

Ethical hacking follows a **structured approach to security testing**, known as the **five phases of hacking**.

17.3.1 Phase 1: Reconnaissance (Information Gathering)

Collects intelligence about **target systems, networks, and employees**.

Uses **open-source intelligence (OSINT), social engineering, and network scanning**.

Tools: **Maltego, Google Dorking, Shodan, FOCA**.

17.3.2 Phase 2: Scanning and Enumeration

Identifies **open ports, vulnerabilities, and network misconfigurations**.

Uses **vulnerability scanners, network mapping tools, and automated scripts**.

Tools: **Nmap, Nessus, Nikto, Burp Suite, Netcat**.

17.3.3 Phase 3: Exploitation (Gaining Access)

Ethical hackers attempt to **exploit vulnerabilities in systems and applications**.

Uses **buffer overflow attacks, SQL injection, privilege escalation, and brute-force attacks**.

Tools: **Metasploit, SQLmap, Hydra, John the Ripper**.

17.3.4 Phase 4: Maintaining Access (Persistence Testing)

Tests whether **attackers can maintain unauthorized access** after initial exploitation.

Uses **backdoors, rootkits, keyloggers, and persistence mechanisms**.

Tools: **Mimikatz, Cobalt Strike, Empire Framework**.

17.3.5 Phase 5: Covering Tracks and Reporting

Ethical hackers **ensure forensic evidence is preserved** for incident analysis.

Generates **detailed penetration testing reports**, documenting findings and remediation strategies.

Ethical hackers **never hide their activities** from system owners and always report findings **transparently**.

17.4 Common Ethical Hacking Techniques

17.4.1 Social Engineering Attacks

Manipulating individuals into revealing **sensitive information or credentials**.

Includes **phishing, pretexting, baiting, and impersonation attacks**.

Tools: **SET (Social Engineering Toolkit), Evilginx2, GoPhish**.

17.4.2 Web Application Penetration Testing

Identifies vulnerabilities in **web applications and APIs**.

Includes **Cross-Site Scripting (XSS), SQL Injection, and Broken Authentication attacks**.

Tools: **Burp Suite, OWASP ZAP, Dirbuster**.

17.4.3 Wireless Network Penetration Testing

Tests **Wi-Fi networks for encryption weaknesses and rogue access points**.

Includes **WPA cracking, Evil Twin attacks, and MAC address spoofing**.

Tools: **Aircrack-ng, Kismet, Wifite**.

17.4.4 Mobile Security Testing

Identifies **security flaws in Android and iOS applications**.

Includes **reverse engineering mobile apps, analyzing insecure APIs, and bypassing root detection**.

Tools: **MobSF, Frida, Drozer, Apktool**.

Ethical hackers must use **authorized testing methods** and **avoid unauthorized exploitation** to maintain integrity.

17.5 Legal and Ethical Considerations in Cybersecurity

Ethical hacking must be conducted **within the framework of cybersecurity laws** and **ethical hacking guidelines**.

17.5.1 Cybersecurity Laws and Regulations

Law	Jurisdiction	Key Provisions
Computer Fraud and Abuse Act (CFAA)	United States	Criminalizes **unauthorized access to computer systems.**
General Data Protection Regulation (GDPR)	European Union	Regulates **data privacy and ethical security assessments.**
Cybercrime Prevention Act	Global	Criminalizes **hacking, identity theft, and cyber fraud.**
Digital Millennium Copyright Act (DMCA)	United States	Restricts **reverse engineering and security research on copyrighted systems.**

Ethical hackers must obtain **written authorization** before conducting penetration tests, ensuring compliance with **cyber laws and industry regulations**.

17.5.2 The Ethics of Cybersecurity Testing

- **Do No Harm:** Ethical hackers must never **damage, alter, or disrupt systems** during testing.
- **Obtain Proper Consent:** Security testing must be **fully authorized by system owners**.
- **Report Vulnerabilities Responsibly:** Ethical hackers must disclose **findings only to authorized parties**.
- **Avoid Exploiting Found Vulnerabilities:** Penetration testers must **never misuse security flaws for personal gain**.

Ethical hacking requires **honesty, transparency, and strict adherence to cybersecurity laws**.

17.6 How to Become an Ethical Hacker

Cybersecurity professionals can enter the field of **ethical hacking and penetration testing** by developing **technical expertise, obtaining certifications, and gaining hands-on experience.**

17.6.1 Steps to Becoming an Ethical Hacker

1. **Develop Strong Networking and Security Knowledge**

- Learn **TCP/IP, DNS, firewalls, and VPN security.**
- Study **Linux and Windows security fundamentals.**

1. **Master Penetration Testing Tools and Techniques**

- Practice using **Kali Linux, Metasploit, Burp Suite, and Wireshark.**
- Participate in **Capture The Flag (CTF) competitions and bug bounty programs.**

1. **Obtain Ethical Hacking Certifications**

- **Certified Ethical Hacker (CEH)** – Covers penetration testing fundamentals.
- **Offensive Security Certified Professional (OSCP)** – Teaches advanced hacking techniques.
- **GIAC Penetration Tester (GPEN)** – Focuses on ethical hacking methodologies.

1. **Gain Hands-On Experience in Security Testing**

- Work in **SOC teams, red teams, or ethical hacking firms.**
- Contribute to **open-source security projects and responsible disclosure programs.**

1. **Stay Updated on Emerging Cyber Threats**

- Follow cybersecurity news, research papers, and exploit databases.
- Engage in **ethical hacking forums and professional security communities**.

A career in ethical hacking offers **high earning potential, continuous learning opportunities, and the ability to protect organizations from cyber threats**.

Conclusion

Ethical hacking is a **critical component of modern cybersecurity**, ensuring organizations **identify vulnerabilities before cybercriminals exploit them**. However, ethical hackers must **operate within legal frameworks, follow responsible disclosure policies, and adhere to ethical hacking best practices**.

In **Chapter 18: Red Team vs. Blue Team Cybersecurity Operations**, we will explore **how offensive and defensive security teams collaborate to strengthen cybersecurity infrastructures**.

Chapter 18

RED TEAM VS. BLUE TEAM CYBERSECURITY OPERATIONS

18.1 Introduction to Red Team and Blue Team Cybersecurity

Cybersecurity operations rely on **proactive and reactive security measures** to protect organizations from cyber threats. **Red teams** and **blue teams** are essential components of this defense strategy, simulating **offensive cyber attacks and defensive security responses** to identify vulnerabilities and strengthen cyber resilience.

- **Red Teams** simulate **real-world cyber threats**, attempting to **breach an organization's security defenses using advanced penetration testing techniques, social engineering, and exploit development**.
- **Blue Teams** defend against **simulated cyber attacks by detecting, responding to, and mitigating security incidents in real-time**.

The interaction between **red teams and blue teams** allows organizations to develop **robust security infrastructures, improve incident response capabilities, and test cybersecurity defense strategies** against evolving attack methodologies.

18.2 The Role of Red Team Cybersecurity Operations

Red teams conduct **authorized cyber attack simulations** to expose security weaknesses in **networks, applications, and human-based security controls**. These operations **mirror the tactics, techniques, and procedures (TTPs) used by real-world adversaries**, helping organizations **strengthen their security postures before actual cybercriminals exploit vulnerabilities**.

18.2.1 Key Responsibilities of a Red Team

1. **Reconnaissance and Information Gathering**

- Uses **open-source intelligence (OSINT), network scanning, and social engineering** to identify attack vectors.
- Tools: **Maltego, Shodan, FOCA, Google Dorking**.

1. **Exploitation and Privilege Escalation**

- Attempts to **exploit system vulnerabilities and escalate privileges to gain deeper access**.
- Tools: **Metasploit, PowerSploit, Cobalt Strike, Empire**.

1. **Persistence and Lateral Movement**

- Deploys **backdoors, rootkits, and credential dumping techniques** to maintain long-term system access.
- Techniques: **Pass-the-Hash, Kerberoasting, LSASS Memory Dumping**.

1. **Data Exfiltration and Impact Analysis**

- Simulates **real-world data theft scenarios**, demonstrating the consequences of a security breach.
- Tools: **Exfiltration over DNS, ICMP Tunneling, Rclone for Cloud Storage**

Exfiltration.

1. **Reporting and Attack Debriefing**

· Provides **detailed reports on exploited vulnerabilities, security miscon-figurations, and remediation steps**.

Red teams **operate under strict ethical guidelines** to ensure that all security testing is **authorized, controlled, and conducted without causing actual harm to systems or data integrity**.

18.3 The Role of Blue Team Cybersecurity Operations

Blue teams are responsible for **detecting, responding to, and mitigating cyber threats** in real time. They utilize **advanced security monitoring, threat intelligence, and forensic analysis** to defend against **malicious actors and simulated red team attacks**.

18.3.1 Key Responsibilities of a Blue Team

1. **Security Monitoring and Threat Detection**

· Uses **Security Information and Event Management (SIEM) platforms to monitor real-time security logs**.
· Tools: **Splunk, ELK Stack, IBM QRadar, Microsoft Sentinel.**

1. **Incident Response and Threat Containment**

· Investigates security alerts, **isolates compromised systems, and implements rapid response actions**.
· Frameworks: **NIST Incident Response Framework, MITRE ATT&CK, Cyber Kill Chain.**

1. **Vulnerability Management and Patch Deployment**

- Identifies and mitigates **exploitable vulnerabilities before attackers can use them**.
- Tools: **Nessus, Qualys, OpenVAS**.

1. **User Awareness Training and Security Hardening**

- Conducts **phishing simulations, security awareness programs, and access control audits** to prevent human errors.

1. **Post-Incident Analysis and Continuous Improvement**

- Analyzes past incidents to **improve defensive strategies and reduce future attack risks**.

Blue teams must **continuously adapt their security defenses to stay ahead of evolving attack techniques**, ensuring **real-time protection against cyber threats**.

18.4 Purple Teaming: Bridging the Gap Between Red and Blue Teams

Purple teaming combines **red team offensive strategies with blue team defensive measures**, fostering **collaborative security testing**. Instead of operating as **separate entities**, red and blue teams **share real-time attack data, threat intelligence, and defensive insights to enhance overall cybersecurity resilience**.

18.4.1 How Purple Teaming Improves Cybersecurity

- **Real–Time Attack Simulations:** Red teams execute **controlled cyber attacks**, while blue teams **respond and adjust defenses in real time**.
- **Shared Intelligence and Defense Optimization:** Blue teams learn from **red team exploits**, improving **threat detection capabilities**.
- **Continuous Security Testing:** Ensures **constant adaptation to new threats and evolving attack methodologies**.

Organizations integrating **purple teaming strategies** benefit from **stronger security postures, enhanced incident response readiness, and proactive cyber risk mitigation**.

18.5 Advanced Red Team vs. Blue Team Attack and Defense Scenarios

Red and blue teams engage in **realistic cybersecurity war games** to test **attack resilience and response effectiveness**.

18.5.1 Red Team Attack Scenarios

Attack Scenario	Red Team Tactics Used
Spear-Phishing Attack on Executives	Delivers malicious email payloads using social engineering.
Internal Network Compromise	Uses privilege escalation and lateral movement to access confidential data.
Ransomware Deployment Simulation	Encrypts test systems to evaluate incident response effectiveness.
Cloud Infrastructure Breach	Exploits misconfigured AWS, Azure, or Google Cloud resources.

18.5.2 Blue Team Defensive Countermeasures

Defense Strategy	Blue Team Countermeasure Used
Anti-Phishing Protection	Deploys email filtering, user training, and AI-powered phishing detection.
Intrusion Detection and Threat Hunting	Uses SIEM platforms and AI-driven anomaly detection.
Ransomware Mitigation	Implements air-gapped backups, endpoint protection, and zero-trust security policies.
Cloud Security Monitoring	Uses CSPM (Cloud Security Posture Management) tools to detect misconfigurations.

By engaging in **live attack simulations and real-time security responses**, organizations gain **actionable insights into cyber risks and strengthen their overall security infrastructure**.

18.6 How to Become a Red Team or Blue Team Cybersecurity Expert

Cybersecurity professionals can specialize in **red team offensive security testing or blue team defensive security operations** by **developing technical expertise, obtaining certifications, and gaining hands-on experience**.

18.6.1 Career Path for Red Team Professionals

1. **Learn Ethical Hacking and Penetration Testing**

- Master **network penetration testing, exploit development, and reverse engineering**.
- Certifications: **OSCP, CEH, GPEN, CRTO (Certified Red Team Operator)**.

1. **Develop Advanced Exploitation Skills**

- Learn **buffer overflow attacks, privilege escalation, and adversary simulation techniques**.

1. **Gain Hands-On Red Team Experience**

· Participate in **Capture The Flag (CTF) challenges, bug bounty programs, and penetration testing projects**.

18.6.2 Career Path for Blue Team Professionals

1. **Develop Threat Detection and Incident Response Skills**

· Learn **SOC monitoring, malware analysis, and forensic investigations**.
· Certifications: **CISSP, GCIH, CySA+, Splunk Certified SOC Analyst**.

1. **Master Security Automation and SIEM Platforms**

· Gain expertise in **log analysis, AI-based threat detection, and SIEM platform configuration**.

1. **Work in Blue Team Cyber Defense Roles**

· Apply for **SOC analyst, incident responder, or threat intelligence roles**.

Specializing in **red team or blue team operations** offers **high-paying job opportunities, career advancement, and the ability to protect organizations from cyber threats**.

Conclusion

Red team and blue team cybersecurity operations are **essential components of proactive cyber defense**. While **red teams expose vulnerabilities by simulating real-world cyber attacks, blue teams defend organizations by detecting and mitigating security incidents in real time**. The rise of **AI-driven cyber warfare, adaptive malware, and nation-state cyber threats** makes **red team vs. blue team cybersecurity strategies critical for modern organizations**.

In **Chapter 19: Cybersecurity in Artificial Intelligence and Machine Learn-**

ing, we will explore **how AI enhances cybersecurity defenses, automates threat detection, and predicts cyber attacks using machine learning models**.

Chapter 19

CYBERSECURITY IN ARTIFICIAL INTELLIGENCE AND MACHINE LEARNING

19.1 Introduction to AI and Machine Learning in Cybersecurity

Artificial Intelligence (AI) and Machine Learning (ML) are revolutionizing cybersecurity by enabling **automated threat detection, real-time security analysis, and predictive defense mechanisms**. These technologies **analyze massive amounts of threat data, detect anomalies, and respond to cyber threats with minimal human intervention**.

However, AI is also being weaponized by cybercriminals to develop **evasive malware, deepfake-based fraud, automated phishing campaigns, and AI-generated cyberattacks**. The rise of **adversarial AI, algorithm poisoning, and deepfake manipulation** presents new cybersecurity challenges that require **advanced AI-driven security defenses**.

This chapter explores the **role of AI in cybersecurity, how machine learning enhances cyber defense, and the growing risks of AI-powered cyber attacks**.

19.2 How AI Enhances Cybersecurity Defense

AI and ML-powered security systems provide **automated, intelligent defense mechanisms** that continuously improve as they **analyze, detect, and neutralize cyber threats**.

19.2.1 Key Benefits of AI in Cybersecurity

1. **Automated Threat Detection**

- AI analyzes real-time security logs and **identifies anomalies that indicate potential cyber threats.**
- Uses **machine learning models to recognize attack patterns and predict future attacks.**

1. **Advanced Malware Detection**

- AI-powered antivirus software **detects new malware variants based on behavioral analysis rather than signature matching.**
- Tools: **Cylance, Darktrace, SentinelOne.**

1. **Behavioral Biometrics and Identity Security**

- AI-driven authentication systems analyze **keystrokes, facial recognition, and voice patterns** to detect identity fraud.
- Used in **multi-factor authentication (MFA) and zero-trust security architectures.**

1. **AI-Driven Security Automation**

- Automates **incident response workflows**, reducing the need for manual intervention.
- Uses **Security Orchestration, Automation, and Response (SOAR) platforms** to detect, analyze, and contain cyber threats.

AI significantly enhances **cybersecurity efficiency, allowing organizations to identify and neutralize threats faster than traditional security approaches.**

19.3 Machine Learning in Cybersecurity: How It Works

Machine Learning (ML) enables cybersecurity systems to **learn from past security incidents, recognize attack patterns, and predict emerging cyber threats**.

19.3.1 Machine Learning Models in Cybersecurity

ML Model	Function in Cybersecurity	Use Case Example
Supervised Learning	Trained on labeled data to recognize **known cyber threats.**	Detects **known malware families and phishing emails.**
Unsupervised Learning	Identifies unknown attack patterns without pre-labeled data.	Detects **zero-day exploits and advanced persistent threats (APTs).**
Reinforcement Learning	AI agents **learn through trial and error,** improving response strategies.	Enhances **automated cyber threat detection and response.**

19.3.2 Applications of Machine Learning in Cybersecurity

1. **AI-Driven Intrusion Detection Systems (IDS)**

- Uses **behavioral analysis to detect anomalies in network traffic.**
- Tools: **Zeek, Snort, AI-powered SIEMs.**

1. **Fraud Detection and Financial Security**

- AI models identify **suspicious financial transactions and credit card fraud** in real time.
- Used by **banks, financial institutions, and payment processors.**

1. **Deep Learning for Malware Classification**

- AI analyzes **malware behavior at the binary level**, identifying previously unknown malware strains.

Machine learning continuously **evolves based on real-world cyber threat data**, making it a critical asset in modern cybersecurity defenses.

19.4 AI-Powered Cyber Threats and Adversarial AI

While AI strengthens cybersecurity, cybercriminals are also using AI to **develop sophisticated attack strategies, evade detection, and automate cybercrime**.

19.4.1 How Cybercriminals Use AI in Attacks

- **AI-Generated Deepfake Scams:** Attackers use **deepfake voice and video manipulation** to impersonate executives and commit fraud.
- **AI-Powered Phishing Attacks:** AI analyzes social media and corporate emails to **generate highly convincing phishing messages**.
- **Adversarial Machine Learning Attacks:** Hackers manipulate **AI models by injecting false data, causing security systems to misclassify threats**.
- **AI-Enhanced Malware Development:** AI-powered malware adapts **in real time**, changing behavior to evade traditional antivirus detection.

19.4.2 Adversarial AI Techniques Used by Cybercriminals

1. **Data Poisoning Attacks**

- Attackers inject **malicious data into machine learning models** to **alter AI behavior and compromise detection accuracy**.

1. **Evasion Attacks**

- AI-powered malware **learns how security systems detect threats** and automatically adjusts its attack methods to avoid detection.

1. **Model Inversion Attacks**

- Hackers extract **sensitive information from AI models**, reconstructing training data to steal user credentials or proprietary data.

Organizations must implement **AI-driven cybersecurity defenses to counter AI-powered attacks**, ensuring that adversarial AI does not **undermine cybersecurity resilience**.

19.5 AI in Cyber Threat Intelligence and Automated Incident Response

AI-powered security systems enhance **threat intelligence gathering, incident response automation, and predictive threat modeling**.

19.5.1 AI in Cyber Threat Intelligence

- **Dark Web Monitoring:** AI scans **darknet marketplaces and cybercriminal forums** for leaked credentials and data breaches.
- **Malware Attribution:** AI analyzes **attack signatures to trace cyber attacks back to their origin**.

19.5.2 AI in Automated Incident Response

- **Security Orchestration, Automation, and Response (SOAR):** AI-powered platforms automate **incident detection, analysis, and mitigation**.
- **Real-Time Threat Containment:** AI isolates compromised systems **before an attack spreads across networks**.

AI-powered cybersecurity solutions **reduce incident response times, automate security tasks, and provide real-time threat intelligence**.

19.6 AI and Blockchain Integration for Cybersecurity

The combination of AI and blockchain enhances **security, transparency, and data integrity** in cybersecurity operations.

19.6.1 Blockchain for AI Model Security

- Ensures **AI model integrity by storing training data on an immutable blockchain ledger**.
- Prevents **adversarial AI attacks and model manipulation**.

19.6.2 AI for Blockchain Security

- AI detects **anomalies in blockchain transactions**, preventing fraud and smart contract exploits.
- AI-enhanced **blockchain security monitors decentralized finance (DeFi) platforms for suspicious activities**.

AI and blockchain **work together to create tamper-proof, automated cyber-security defense mechanisms**.

19.7 Ethical and Legal Challenges of AI in Cybersecurity

AI-driven cybersecurity presents **ethical, legal, and regulatory challenges**, including **data privacy concerns, AI bias, and the risks of autonomous cyber attacks**.

19.7.1 Ethical Challenges of AI in Cybersecurity

- **Bias in AI Decision-Making:** AI security models may exhibit **biases, leading to false positives or misclassifications**.
- **AI-Powered Mass Surveillance:** Governments and corporations use AI to **monitor online activities, raising privacy concerns**.

- **Autonomous AI-Driven Cyber Attacks:** Cybercriminals can deploy AI-powered **self-replicating malware that evolves autonomously**.

19.7.2 Legal and Compliance Challenges

- **AI in GDPR and Data Protection Regulations:** AI-driven security solutions must comply with **privacy laws that govern automated decision-making**.
- **Legal Responsibility for AI Security Decisions:** Organizations must define **accountability for AI-driven cybersecurity decisions and false positives**.

Governments and enterprises must **develop AI governance policies** to ensure that AI-powered cybersecurity remains **ethical, transparent, and legally compliant**.

Conclusion

AI and machine learning are transforming **cybersecurity by enhancing threat detection, automating incident response, and enabling predictive cyber defense mechanisms**. However, the rise of **AI-powered cyber attacks, adversarial AI, and deepfake-driven fraud** requires organizations to **develop AI-driven countermeasures and enforce strict AI governance policies**.

In **Chapter 20: Cybersecurity in Smart Cities and Critical Infrastructure**, we will explore **the security challenges of IoT-enabled smart cities, industrial control systems (ICS), and the protection of national critical infrastructure from cyber threats**.

Chapter 20

CYBERSECURITY IN SMART CITIES AND CRITICAL INFRASTRUCTURE

20.1 Introduction to Smart City and Critical Infrastructure Security

Smart cities integrate **Internet of Things (IoT) devices, artificial intelligence (AI), and connected infrastructure** to enhance urban efficiency, sustainability, and public safety. However, as **critical infrastructure becomes increasingly digitized and automated, the risk of cyber threats targeting power grids, transportation systems, water supplies, and emergency services escalates**.

Cybersecurity in smart cities and critical infrastructure requires **advanced security frameworks, real-time monitoring, and proactive threat mitigation** to prevent **nation-state attacks, ransomware incidents, and infrastructure sabotage**. Governments, security professionals, and technology providers must implement **robust cybersecurity policies, zero-trust architectures, and AI-driven security automation** to protect essential services from cyber disruptions.

20.2 Smart City Cybersecurity Risks and Challenges

Smart cities rely on **massive data exchanges between IoT sensors, cloud platforms, and AI-driven automation systems**, creating multiple **attack surfaces for cybercriminals**.

20.2.1 Common Cybersecurity Threats in Smart Cities

1. **IoT Device Vulnerabilities**

- Unsecured IoT sensors and smart devices **can be hijacked, manipulated, or used as botnet nodes**.
- Tools: **Mirai Botnet, IoTReaper, Mozi Malware**.

1. **Infrastructure Sabotage via Cyber Attacks**

- Attackers can **disable smart traffic lights, cause grid failures, or manipulate water treatment plants**.
- Example: **Ukraine Power Grid Attack (2015) – Russian hackers shut down electricity for 230,000 people**.

1. **Data Breaches and Privacy Violations**

- Smart city surveillance systems **collect biometric, facial recognition, and real-time location data**, increasing privacy concerns.

1. **Cloud and Edge Computing Security Risks**

- Cloud-based infrastructure is **vulnerable to misconfigurations, unauthorized access, and data interception**.
- Tools: **Shodan, Censys, OpenCloud Security Scanners**.

1. **Ransomware and Extortion Attacks on City Systems**

- Ransomware operators target **municipal IT networks, hospitals, and emergency response systems**, demanding ransom payments.
- Example: **Baltimore Ransomware Attack (2019) – $18 million in damages after city services were paralyzed**.

Smart city cybersecurity requires **multi-layered defense strategies, strict IoT security policies, and AI-driven real-time monitoring** to prevent cyber attacks.

20.3 Securing Critical Infrastructure from Cyber Attacks

Critical infrastructure includes **power grids, water treatment plants, transportation networks, healthcare facilities, and emergency services**. Disruptions to these systems **can have catastrophic consequences**.

20.3.1 Common Cyber Threats to Critical Infrastructure

1. **Industrial Control System (ICS) Exploits**

- Attackers target **Supervisory Control and Data Acquisition (SCADA) systems** to manipulate industrial processes.
- Example: **Stuxnet (2010) – A sophisticated cyber weapon used to sabotage Iran's nuclear centrifuges**.

1. **Rogue Nation-State Cyber Attacks**

- Nation-state hackers infiltrate **energy grids, financial systems, and government agencies** to disrupt national security.
- Example: **NotPetya (2017) – Russian-linked ransomware attack caused $10 billion in global damages**.

1. **DDoS Attacks Against Emergency Services**

- Cybercriminals **overload 911 call centers, disrupt hospital networks, and disable fire department communication systems**.
- Example: **Israeli Emergency System DDoS Attack (2020) – Disrupted national emergency lines for hours**.

1. **Supply Chain Attacks on Critical Infrastructure Providers**

- Attackers infiltrate **third-party vendors and contractors** to deploy **backdoors and malware into critical infrastructure networks**.
- Example: **SolarWinds Attack (2020) – Russian APT compromised U.S. government agencies and tech companies via supply chain infiltration**.

To secure critical infrastructure, organizations must implement **zero-trust security models, network segmentation, and AI-driven intrusion detection systems**.

20.4 Best Practices for Smart City and Critical Infrastructure Cybersecurity

20.4.1 Implementing Zero-Trust Security in Smart Cities

- **Zero-trust architecture** assumes that all network activity is **potentially malicious** and requires continuous authentication.
- Uses **multi-factor authentication (MFA), behavior-based access controls, and AI-driven anomaly detection**.

20.4.2 Hardening IoT Security for Smart Cities

- **Enforce Strong IoT Device Authentication**Require **unique device credentials and secure certificate-based authentication**.
- **Apply Firmware and Security Patching**Regularly update IoT firmware to **patch vulnerabilities and prevent exploitation**.
- **Segment IoT Networks from Critical IT Systems**Prevent attackers from

moving laterally across smart city networks.

20.4.3 Strengthening Cyber Resilience in Critical Infrastructure

1. **AI-Powered Threat Detection and Monitoring**

- Deploys **machine learning algorithms to detect abnormal activity in power grids, water systems, and transportation networks.**
- Tools: **Darktrace AI, Splunk, IBM Watson Security.**

1. **Secure Industrial Control Systems (ICS) and SCADA Environments**

- Implement **intrusion detection systems (IDS) to monitor industrial networks for cyber threats.**
- Tools: **Dragos, Nozomi Networks, Claroty.**

1. **Conduct Cybersecurity Drills and Red Team Simulations**

- Regularly test infrastructure resilience against **simulated cyber attacks and penetration testing exercises.**

1. **Backup and Disaster Recovery Planning**

- Maintain **air-gapped backups** to prevent ransomware from corrupting critical infrastructure data.

Governments and enterprises must **continuously evolve cybersecurity policies to safeguard national critical infrastructure from digital threats.**

20.5 Government Regulations and Cybersecurity Compliance for Critical Infrastructure

20.5.1 Key Cybersecurity Regulations for Smart Cities and Critical Infrastructure

Regulation	Jurisdiction	Focus Area
NIST Cybersecurity Framework	United States	Guidelines for securing critical infrastructure and industrial control systems.
European Union NIS Directive	European Union	Regulates smart city and critical infrastructure cybersecurity.
ISO/IEC 27001	Global	Establishes best practices for securing IT and industrial networks.
CISA National Critical Infrastructure Protection Plan	United States	Protects transportation, energy, and emergency services from cyber threats.

20.5.2 Government-Led Cybersecurity Initiatives

- **United States Cybersecurity and Infrastructure Security Agency (CISA)**
  – Protects national critical infrastructure from cyber attacks.
- **European Cyber Resilience Act (CRA)** – Strengthens **smart city and IoT security standards**.
- **China's Cybersecurity Law** – Implements **strict security controls for industrial automation and critical sectors**.

Smart cities and critical infrastructure operators must comply with **government-mandated cybersecurity regulations** to prevent **cyber incidents and infrastructure disruptions**.

20.6 Future Trends in Smart City and Critical Infrastructure Cybersecurity

As **smart cities and critical infrastructure continue evolving**, cybersecurity strategies must **adapt to emerging threats and technological advancements**.

20.6.1 Emerging Technologies in Cybersecurity for Smart Cities

- **Quantum Cryptography for Smart City Networks**Ensures **unbreakable encryption for IoT, cloud, and AI-driven urban infrastructure**.
- **5G Security and Zero-Trust Edge Computing**Protects **5G-powered smart city applications from cyber espionage and network manipulation**.
- **AI-Driven Autonomous Cyber Defense**Uses AI-powered security automation **to detect, neutralize, and prevent cyber threats in real time**.

Future smart cities and critical infrastructure must **incorporate cutting-edge cybersecurity solutions to defend against evolving cyber threats**.

Conclusion

Cybersecurity in **smart cities and critical infrastructure** is essential to **protect public services, transportation, energy grids, and emergency systems** from cyber threats. As **cybercriminals, hacktivists, and nation-state adversaries target urban infrastructure**, governments and organizations must **implement AI-driven security automation, zero-trust architectures, and advanced threat intelligence**.

In **Chapter 21: The Dark Web and Cybercrime Markets**, we will explore **how cybercriminals operate on the dark web, the tools they use, and the role of anonymous marketplaces in cybercrime**.

Chapter 21

THE DARK WEB AND CYBERCRIME MARKETS

21.1 Introduction to the Dark Web and Cybercrime Economy

The **dark web** is an encrypted section of the internet that is **not indexed by standard search engines** and requires specialized software such as **Tor (The Onion Router) or I2P (Invisible Internet Project) to access**. While the dark web provides **privacy and anonymity for journalists, whistleblowers, and political dissidents**, it is also **a hub for cybercrime, illicit trade, and underground markets**.

Cybercriminals leverage the dark web for **buying and selling stolen data, hacking tools, ransomware-as-a-service (RaaS), and illicit services**. The dark web's **unregulated nature and anonymous transactions** make it a significant challenge for **law enforcement, cybersecurity professionals, and financial institutions** attempting to combat cybercrime.

This chapter explores **how cybercriminals operate on the dark web, the structure of cybercrime marketplaces, the tools used for anonymity, and law enforcement strategies for tracking illegal activities**.

21.2 Structure of the Dark Web and Cybercriminal Networks

The internet is divided into **three primary layers**, each serving different purposes.

21.2.1 The Three Layers of the Internet

Internet Layer	Accessibility	Common Use Cases
Surface Web	Indexed by search engines	Websites such as Google, Amazon, Wikipedia
Deep Web	Requires login credentials or private access	Online banking, academic databases, private forums
Dark Web	Requires specialized software (Tor, I2P)	Anonymous communication, underground markets, illicit services

The **dark web's encrypted structure** allows users to **browse anonymously**, making it a preferred environment for cybercriminals engaging in **illegal trade, financial fraud, and cyber warfare operations**.

21.3 Cybercrime Markets and Illicit Goods on the Dark Web

Dark web marketplaces operate similarly to **e-commerce platforms**, featuring **vendor listings, product descriptions, escrow payment systems, and customer reviews**. However, instead of legal goods, these platforms specialize in **stolen data, hacking tools, and illegal services**.

21.3.1 Types of Cybercrime Marketplaces

Dark Web Marketplaces (DWM)

Function like **black-market versions of Amazon or eBay**.

Sell **stolen credit cards, counterfeit documents, and hacking services**.

Examples: **Silk Road (shutdown), AlphaBay (shutdown), Hydra Market (shutdown), DarkFox Market (active)**.

Ransomware-as-a-Service (RaaS) Platforms

Provide **pre-built ransomware kits** to cybercriminals who lack technical skills.

Operators take a **percentage of ransomware profits** from affiliates.

Examples: **LockBit RaaS, Conti RaaS, REvil RaaS**.

Fraud and Financial Crime Forums

Facilitate **identity theft, credit card fraud, and bank fraud techniques**.

Distribute **stolen financial data, cloned ATM cards, and fake PayPal accounts**.

Examples: **CardPlanet, Joker's Stash, Rescator, Genesis Market**.

Exploit and Zero-Day Marketplaces

Sell **undisclosed vulnerabilities (zero-days) to cybercriminals, governments, and private buyers**.

Buyers use these exploits for **cyber warfare, espionage, or corporate sabotage**.

Examples: **Zerodium, Exodus Intelligence, Shadow Brokers (shutdown)**.

Stolen Data and Credential Dump Sites

Offer **hacked databases, login credentials, and compromised email accounts**.

Some operate as **subscription-based services providing real-time breached data**.

Examples: **BreachForums, RaidForums (shutdown), ShinyHunters**.

The **dark web economy thrives on anonymity**, making it difficult for authorities to track illicit transactions and dismantle cybercrime networks.

21.4 Anonymity Tools Used by Cybercriminals on the Dark Web

Cybercriminals use **various technologies and techniques** to maintain anonymity while engaging in **illegal activities on the dark web**.

21.4.1 Key Anonymity Tools and Techniques

Tor (The Onion Router)

Routes traffic through **multiple encrypted nodes**, obscuring user identity.

Used for **browsing dark web marketplaces and communicating anonymously**.

I2P (Invisible Internet Project)

Provides **peer-to-peer encrypted networking**, similar to Tor but with greater decentralization.

Cryptocurrency for Untraceable Payments

Bitcoin (BTC), Monero (XMR), and Zcash (ZEC) are commonly used for **anonymous transactions**.

Monero is favored due to **privacy-focused blockchain transactions**.

Bulletproof Hosting Services

Provide **untraceable server hosting for cybercriminal websites, hacking forums, and malware command-and-control (C2) servers**.

Located in **jurisdictions that do not cooperate with law enforcement**.

PGP Encryption and Secure Messaging Apps

Criminals use **Pretty Good Privacy (PGP) encryption** to secure communications.

Encrypted messaging apps: **Signal, Wickr, Tox**.

These anonymity tools make it **challenging for law enforcement agencies to track and dismantle cybercriminal organizations**.

21.5 Law Enforcement Operations Against Dark Web Cybercrime

Governments and cybersecurity agencies deploy **advanced tracking, de-anonymization, and cyber-infiltration techniques** to combat cybercrime on the dark web.

21.5.1 Major Law Enforcement Operations Targeting Dark Web Markets

Operation	Year	Impact
Operation Onymous	2014	Shutdown of Silk Road 2.0, Cloud 9, Hydra, and other marketplaces.
Operation Bayonet	2017	Shutdown of AlphaBay and Hansa Market.
Operation DisrupTor	2020	179 arrests and seizure of 500+ dark web vendor accounts.
Genesis Market Takedown	2023	Seizure of Genesis Market, a major stolen credentials marketplace.

21.5.2 Cybercrime Tracking Techniques Used by Authorities

- **Blockchain Analysis and Crypto Tracking**Investigators use **Chainalysis, CipherTrace, and Elliptic** to **trace cryptocurrency transactions** on the dark web.
- **Traffic Deanonymization and Network Surveillance**Agencies deploy **machine learning models to detect and unmask Tor network traffic**.
- **Undercover Cybercrime Infiltration**Law enforcement infiltrates **hacking forums and dark web marketplaces** to gather intelligence and identify criminals.

Despite these efforts, **cybercriminals continuously adapt, using new techniques to evade detection**, requiring law enforcement to **constantly evolve their cybercrime tracking methods**.

21.6 The Future of Dark Web Cybercrime and Countermeasures

As cybersecurity advances, cybercriminals are developing **more sophisticated dark web operations**, requiring organizations and governments to adopt **next-generation cyber defense strategies**.

21.6.1 Emerging Trends in Dark Web Cybercrime

- **AI-Generated Fraud and Deepfake Scams**Cybercriminals use **AI-generated deepfake voices and videos** to commit fraud.
- **Quantum-Resistant Cryptocurrency for Untraceable Payments**Future dark web markets may transition to **quantum-resistant cryptocurrencies**.
- **AI-Powered Dark Web Marketplaces**Automated **AI-driven cybercrime services** will increase **attack scale and efficiency**.

21.6.2 Strengthening Cybersecurity Against Dark Web Threats

- **AI-Driven Dark Web Monitoring**Uses **machine learning algorithms to track stolen data, leaked credentials, and illicit activities.**
- **Blockchain-Based Identity Verification**Future regulations may require **traceable, encrypted identity verification for online transactions.**
- **International Law Enforcement Collaboration**Global efforts between **Interpol, Europol, and national cybercrime agencies** are crucial for **disrupting cybercriminal operations.**

Cybercriminals will **continue evolving,** but **governments, cybersecurity professionals, and AI-powered security frameworks will play a critical role in countering dark web cybercrime.**

Conclusion

The **dark web remains a major hub for cybercriminal activity,** enabling **financial fraud, ransomware distribution, identity theft, and hacking services.** While law enforcement agencies **continue to shut down dark web markets and trace illicit transactions,** cybercriminals adapt using **new anonymity tools, AI-powered cybercrime tactics, and quantum-resistant payment systems.**

   In **Chapter 22: Cybersecurity and the Future of Digital Warfare,** we will explore **how cyber warfare is shaping global conflicts, the rise of nation-state cyber attacks, and strategies for defending against digital warfare operations.**

Chapter 22

CYBERSECURITY AND THE FUTURE OF DIGITAL WARFARE

22.1 Introduction to Digital Warfare and Cybersecurity

Cyber warfare has become **a core component of modern military strategy**, where **nation-states, intelligence agencies, and cybercriminal organizations conduct cyber attacks to disrupt governments, economies, and military operations**. Unlike traditional warfare, digital warfare allows **high-impact attacks to be launched remotely, targeting critical infrastructure, financial systems, and defense networks without deploying physical troops**.

The rise of **state-sponsored cyber attacks, cyber espionage, artificial intelligence (AI)-powered warfare, and quantum computing threats** has created an urgent need for **advanced cybersecurity defense mechanisms, real-time threat intelligence, and cyber warfare countermeasures**.

This chapter explores the **landscape of digital warfare, the role of cyber weapons, real-world cyber conflicts, and how nations are preparing for the future of cyber warfare**.

22.2 Cyber Warfare Tactics and Digital Attack Strategies

Cyber warfare operations involve **a combination of cyber espionage, digital sabotage, and cyber-physical attacks** designed to disrupt an adversary's national security, critical infrastructure, and technological capabilities.

22.2.1 Categories of Cyber Warfare Operations

1. **Cyber Espionage and Intelligence Gathering**

- Infiltrates **government agencies, military networks, and corporations** to steal classified data.
- Techniques: **Advanced Persistent Threats (APTs), zero-day exploits, supply chain attacks.**
- Example: **Chinese APT10 hacking campaign targeting global defense contractors and intelligence agencies.**

1. **Critical Infrastructure Attacks**

- Disrupts **power grids, transportation systems, water treatment plants, and financial markets.**
- Example: **Russia's BlackEnergy malware attack on Ukraine's power grid in 2015, causing widespread outages.**

1. **Military Network Disruptions**

- Targets **command-and-control (C2) systems, satellite networks, and secure military communications.**
- Example: **U.S. Cyber Command's takedown of ISIS online propaganda networks using cyber warfare tactics.**

1. **Economic Cyber Warfare**

- Disrupts financial institutions, stock markets, and economic infrastructure through **denial-of-service attacks, ransomware, and financial fraud**.
- Example: **North Korea's Lazarus Group cyber attack on Bangladesh's central bank, stealing $81 million via SWIFT hacking**.

1. **AI-Enhanced Disinformation and Psychological Warfare**

- Uses **AI-generated deepfakes, social media manipulation, and botnet-driven misinformation campaigns** to destabilize political systems.
- Example: **Russian state-backed troll farms influencing U.S. and European elections through social media disinformation campaigns**.

Cyber warfare is evolving from **traditional hacking operations to AI-driven autonomous cyber weapons capable of executing large-scale attacks in real time**.

22.3 Cyber Weapons and Nation-State Cyber Attack Programs

Governments and military agencies **develop cyber weapons to conduct offensive and defensive cyber warfare operations**. Cyber weapons range from **malware designed to destroy industrial systems to AI-powered cyber attack platforms**.

22.3.1 Cyber Weapons Used in Digital Warfare

Cyber Weapon Type	Function	Example
Malware-Based Cyber Weapons	Infect and disrupt target systems.	Stuxnet – Destroyed Iranian nuclear centrifuges using ICS malware.
AI-Powered Cyber Warfare Platforms	Automates cyber attack execution and vulnerability exploitation.	China's AI-driven cyber intelligence units for military cyber operations.
Deepfake and Disinformation Weapons	Manipulates digital media and public perception.	Russian AI-generated deepfake news networks influencing global politics.
Quantum Hacking Programs	Uses quantum computing to break cryptographic security.	U.S. and China's race for quantum supremacy in cyber warfare.

As **cyber warfare technologies advance**, autonomous AI-driven cyber attacks and quantum computing-based decryption will redefine global cybersecurity challenges.

22.4 Case Studies: Real-World Cyber Warfare Attacks

22.4.1 Stuxnet (2010) – The First Cyber Weapon

- **Target:** Iran's nuclear centrifuges at the Natanz facility.
- **Method:** Stuxnet malware infected **SCADA industrial control systems**, causing **physical damage to nuclear centrifuges by altering their operational speeds**.
- **Impact: Set back Iran's nuclear program by several years** and demonstrated the potential of **cyber weapons in military conflict**.

22.4.2 NotPetya (2017) – The Most Devastating Cyber Attack

- **Target:** Global financial systems, corporations, and infrastructure.
- **Method:** Russian-backed cyber attack **disguised as ransomware but designed for destruction**, spreading through **Ukraine's accounting software to global enterprises**.
- **Impact: Over $10 billion in economic damage, disrupting global shipping, banking, and logistics industries**.

22.4.3 SolarWinds Supply Chain Attack (2020)

- **Target:** U.S. government agencies and Fortune 500 companies.
- **Method:** Russian-backed hackers infiltrated **SolarWinds software up-dates, embedding malware to compromise 18,000+ organizations**.
- **Impact: Long-term intelligence compromise of U.S. national security agencies and private corporations.**

These case studies illustrate how **nation-state cyber warfare operations can cause large-scale financial, military, and geopolitical disruptions.**

22.5 Future Threats in Cyber Warfare

The next generation of **cyber warfare threats will involve AI-driven au-tonomous cyber attacks, quantum computing-based cryptographic decryp-tion, and cyber-physical sabotage.**

22.5.1 AI-Powered Autonomous Cyber Weapons

- **AI-driven malware and botnets will autonomously identify and exploit vulnerabilities without human intervention.**
- **Deepfake-powered cyber propaganda campaigns will manipulate public opinion on a global scale.**

22.5.2 Quantum Computing Threats to Cyber Warfare

- **Quantum computers will break existing cryptographic standards, ex-posing classified military communications and financial transactions.**
- **Governments are investing in post-quantum cryptography to mitigate these risks.**

22.5.3 Weaponized IoT and 5G Cyber Attacks

- **IoT-based botnets will be used for mass-scale DDoS attacks against critical infrastructure**.
- **5G-enabled cyber attacks will disrupt smart cities, autonomous vehicles, and AI-driven defense systems**.

Cyber warfare will continue evolving, requiring **nations to develop next-generation cybersecurity defense frameworks, cyber treaties, and AI-enhanced security infrastructures**.

22.6 Cyber Defense Strategies Against Digital Warfare

22.6.1 Cyber Command and Military Cybersecurity Programs

- The **United States Cyber Command (USCYBERCOM)** and other military agencies develop **cyber warfare response teams and offensive cyber capabilities**.
- Countries such as **China, Russia, Israel, and North Korea have advanced cyber warfare divisions** conducting **cyber espionage and state-backed hacking operations**.

22.6.2 AI-Driven Threat Intelligence and Cyber Defense

- Uses **AI-powered cybersecurity platforms to detect and neutralize cyber warfare threats in real time**.
- Deploys **cyber deception techniques, such as honeypots, to mislead attackers**.

22.6.3 International Cybersecurity Alliances and Cyber Treaties

- The **NATO Cooperative Cyber Defense Center of Excellence (CCDCOE) leads global cyber defense cooperation**.
- Governments are **establishing international agreements on cyber warfare rules and restrictions**.

Cyber warfare is now **a permanent component of global security strategy**, requiring **continuous advancements in cybersecurity technology, military cyber defense units, and AI-driven threat detection systems**.

Conclusion

Cyber warfare is **reshaping global conflicts**, where **nation-states deploy cyber weapons, AI-driven cyber attacks, and digital espionage campaigns** to gain military and economic advantages. As **autonomous AI-powered cyber weapons, quantum decryption, and cyber-physical sabotage continue evolving**, nations must **develop next-generation cybersecurity strategies, cyber treaties, and AI-driven threat intelligence systems**.

In **Chapter 23: The Future of Cybersecurity Careers and Ethical Hacking**, we will explore **how cybersecurity professionals can prepare for the future, the impact of AI on cybersecurity jobs, and the evolving role of ethical hacking in global cyber defense**.

Chapter 23

THE FUTURE OF CYBERSECURITY CAREERS AND ETHICAL HACKING

23.1 Introduction to the Future of Cybersecurity Careers

As cyber threats continue to evolve, cybersecurity careers are becoming **one of the most in-demand and high-paying fields** in technology. With the **rise of AI-driven cyber attacks, quantum computing threats, cyber warfare, and expanding global regulations**, the demand for skilled cybersecurity professionals will continue to increase.

Cybersecurity careers are no longer limited to **network security analysts and ethical hackers**. The future of cybersecurity will include **AI security engineers, quantum cryptography specialists, cyber warfare analysts, and blockchain security experts**. This chapter explores **the emerging cybersecurity career paths, the impact of AI on the industry, and how professionals can prepare for the future of ethical hacking and cyber defense**.

23.2 The Future of Cybersecurity Career Opportunities

Cybersecurity is expanding beyond **traditional IT security roles** to include **new specialties in AI security, critical infrastructure protection, decentralized identity verification, and offensive cyber operations**.

23.2.1 Emerging Cybersecurity Job Roles

Job Role	Responsibilities	Future Demand
AI-Powered Security Engineer	Develops AI-driven cyber defense systems and automates threat detection.	High
Quantum Cryptography Specialist	Designs quantum-resistant encryption protocols to protect against quantum computing attacks.	High
Blockchain Security Analyst	Secures decentralized finance (DeFi) platforms, smart contracts, and NFT marketplaces.	High
Cyber Warfare Defense Analyst	Defends military networks from AI-driven cyber threats and nation-state attacks.	Very High
Zero-Trust Security Architect	Implements zero-trust security frameworks for cloud and enterprise systems.	High
Digital Forensics AI Investigator	Uses AI to analyze malware, ransomware, and cybercrime evidence.	High

The cybersecurity workforce will need to **continuously evolve, integrating AI, blockchain, and quantum-resistant security techniques** into modern defense strategies.

23.3 The Impact of AI on Cybersecurity Careers

23.3.1 AI's Role in Cyber Defense

Artificial Intelligence is already **replacing manual security tasks** and transforming the way cybersecurity operations function. Future security professionals will be required to **work alongside AI-driven security systems to detect and respond to threats**.

AI-Powered Threat Intelligence

AI will analyze **millions of cyber threat indicators in real time**, identifying attack patterns faster than human analysts.

Tools: **Darktrace AI, Splunk AI, IBM Watson for Cybersecurity**.

Automated Security Operations Centers (SOC)

AI-driven SOCs will **replace traditional human-based monitoring**, allowing security teams to **focus on higher-level strategy and investigation**.

AI-Powered Incident Response

Machine learning algorithms will **autonomously investigate security incidents, prioritize risks, and initiate defensive actions**.

23.3.2 Will AI Replace Cybersecurity Jobs?

AI will **enhance cybersecurity careers rather than eliminate them**, creating **new job opportunities in AI security engineering, AI-driven threat intelligence, and machine learning-based cyber defense**. However, **cybersecurity professionals will need to develop AI expertise** to remain relevant.

23.4 The Evolution of Ethical Hacking and Penetration Testing

Ethical hacking is **undergoing rapid transformation**, incorporating **AI-assisted penetration testing, automated vulnerability discovery, and real-time red team simulations**.

23.4.1 The Future of Ethical Hacking Tools

Technology	Impact on Ethical Hacking	Example Tools
AI-Driven Exploit Development	AI will autonomously discover and exploit security vulnerabilities.	OpenAI Codex, ChatGPT for Exploit Writing
Automated Red Teaming	AI-powered red teams will conduct continuous attack simulations without human oversight.	Cobalt Strike AI, MITRE CALDERA
Machine Learning-Based Threat Simulation	AI will generate realistic attack traffic for penetration testing and defense analysis.	Infection Monkey, AttackIQ

Ethical hackers must **integrate AI into penetration testing methodologies** while ensuring **AI-driven security assessments remain transparent, accurate, and ethical**.

23.5 Preparing for the Future of Cybersecurity Careers

Cybersecurity professionals must **continuously adapt to new technologies, threat landscapes, and global regulations**.

23.5.1 Essential Skills for Future Cybersecurity Experts

Skill	Application in Cybersecurity
AI and Machine Learning	Used for automating cyber threat detection and AI-driven security analysis.
Quantum Cryptography	Ensures secure encryption in a post-quantum era.
Blockchain and Decentralized Security	Secures smart contracts, DeFi, and decentralized identity verification.
Cyber Warfare Defense Strategies	Defends against nation-state cyber attacks and AI-powered digital warfare.

23.5.2 Future Cybersecurity Certifications and Training

New certifications will be required to **validate cybersecurity expertise in AI security, quantum cryptography, and advanced ethical hacking**.

Certified AI Security Professional (CAISP) – Covers **AI-driven cyber defense, machine learning-based threat intelligence, and adversarial AI security**.

Quantum Cryptography Specialist (QCS) – Focuses on **post-quantum encryption and cryptanalysis**.

Blockchain Security Professional (BSP) – Validates **expertise in DeFi security, smart contract audits, and NFT cybersecurity**.

Cybersecurity professionals must **engage in continuous learning, hands-on training, and cybersecurity research to stay ahead of emerging threats**.

23.6 Cybersecurity Career Salaries and Industry Demand

Cybersecurity remains one of the **highest-paying career fields**, with salaries continuing to increase as demand grows.

23.6.1 Projected Cybersecurity Salaries (2025-2030)

Job Role	Average Salary (USD)
Entry-Level Cybersecurity Analyst	$85,000 – $105,000
Penetration Tester (Ethical Hacker)	$110,000 – $160,000
AI-Powered Security Engineer	$130,000 – $190,000
Cyber Warfare Defense Analyst	$150,000 – $210,000
Chief Information Security Officer (CISO)	$250,000 – $500,000

Cybersecurity professionals with **AI expertise, quantum cryptography knowledge, and cyber warfare defense experience** will have the **highest-paying career opportunities** in the industry.

23.7 The Future of Cybersecurity Workforce Development

Governments, corporations, and educational institutions are investing in **cybersecurity workforce development programs to close the global cybersecurity skills gap**.

23.7.1 Future Cybersecurity Workforce Initiatives

1. **Government-Led Cybersecurity Training Programs**

- The **U.S. Cyber Talent Initiative** and **EU Cyber Resilience Workforce Strategy** are creating **global cybersecurity training pipelines**.

1. **AI-Driven Cybersecurity Education Platforms**

- AI will **personalize cybersecurity training, providing hands-on simulation environments for security professionals**.

1. **Diversity and Inclusion in Cybersecurity**

- Future cybersecurity programs will **increase accessibility for underrepresented groups** to meet the growing demand for cybersecurity experts.

Cybersecurity careers will remain **a high-demand industry, requiring continuous investment in workforce training, AI-driven cybersecurity education, and hands-on cyber defense programs**.

Conclusion

The future of cybersecurity careers will be **driven by AI, quantum cryptography, blockchain security, and cyber warfare defense**. Ethical hacking will evolve **into AI-powered penetration testing, automated red teaming, and machine learning-driven security assessments**.

Cybersecurity professionals must **continuously adapt, develop AI security expertise, and acquire future-focused cybersecurity certifications** to remain competitive in the industry.

In **Chapter 24: The Ultimate Guide to Cybersecurity Mastery**, we will outline **the complete roadmap to becoming a cybersecurity expert, from foundational skills to advanced career specializations**.

Chapter 24

THE ULTIMATE GUIDE TO CYBERSECURITY MASTERY

24.1 Introduction to Cybersecurity Mastery

Cybersecurity mastery requires **a deep understanding of digital security principles, offensive and defensive security techniques, and advanced cyber threat mitigation strategies**. The field is constantly evolving, demanding **continuous learning, hands-on practice, and expertise in emerging technologies such as artificial intelligence, blockchain security, and quantum cryptography**.

This chapter provides **a structured, step-by-step roadmap to achieving cybersecurity mastery**, covering **fundamental skills, advanced training, professional certifications, and career specialization paths**. Whether you are starting in cybersecurity or aiming to become an industry expert, this guide will help you **develop the expertise required to excel in the cybersecurity profession**.

24.2 The Cybersecurity Mastery Roadmap

To master cybersecurity, professionals must **progress through key skill levels**, from foundational knowledge to expert specialization.

24.2.1 The Five Stages of Cybersecurity Mastery

Stage	Focus Areas	Required Skills
Beginner	Learn cybersecurity fundamentals	Networking, Linux, Windows Security, Basic Scripting
Intermediate	Hands-on security analysis and penetration testing	Ethical Hacking, Web Security, Malware Analysis
Advanced	Real-world cybersecurity application	Red Teaming, Threat Hunting, Incident Response
Expert	Specializing in high-demand cybersecurity fields	AI Security, Cyber Warfare, Zero-Trust Security
Mastery	Leading cybersecurity innovations	AI-Powered Defense, Quantum Cryptography, Security Research

Mastering cybersecurity requires **structured learning, hands-on experience, certifications, and real-world application of cybersecurity principles**.

24.3 Cybersecurity Fundamentals: The Essential Knowledge Base

A strong foundation in cybersecurity begins with **core technical skills in networking, operating systems, cryptography, and security frameworks**.

24.3.1 Key Foundational Skills for Cybersecurity

Networking and Protocols

Understand **TCP/IP, DNS, HTTP, VPNs, Firewalls, and Intrusion Detection Systems (IDS)**.

Learn **Wireshark and network traffic analysis tools**.

Linux and Windows Security

Master **Linux command-line security configurations (Kali Linux, Ubuntu Security Hardening)**.

Learn **Windows security policies, Active Directory (AD) exploitation, and PowerShell security tools**.

Programming and Scripting

Learn **Python for security automation, Bash for Linux security, and PowerShell for Windows security**.

Understand **malware scripting and exploit development**.

Cybersecurity Frameworks and Standards

Study **NIST Cybersecurity Framework, CIS Controls, MITRE ATT&CK Framework, and ISO/IEC 27001.**

Mastering these fundamental skills is essential before advancing into **offensive and defensive cybersecurity techniques.**

24.4 Offensive Cybersecurity Mastery: Ethical Hacking and Red Teaming

Offensive security involves **penetration testing, red teaming, and exploit development** to identify and mitigate vulnerabilities before cybercriminals exploit them.

24.4.1 Ethical Hacking Mastery Path

Web Application Penetration Testing

Learn **SQL Injection (SQLi), Cross-Site Scripting (XSS), Cross-Site Request Forgery (CSRF), and Server-Side Request Forgery (SSRF).**

Tools: **Burp Suite, OWASP ZAP, Nikto, Dirbuster.**

Network Penetration Testing

Exploit **firewall misconfigurations, open ports, and insecure network protocols.**

Tools: **Nmap, Metasploit, Netcat, Responder.**

Wireless and IoT Hacking

Test **Wi-Fi networks, Bluetooth devices, and smart home security.**

Tools: **Aircrack-ng, Wireshark, Kismet.**

Privilege Escalation and Post-Exploitation

Learn **Linux and Windows privilege escalation techniques.**

Tools: **Mimikatz, PowerSploit, Empire, Cobalt Strike.**

Red Teaming and Adversarial Simulation

Conduct **real-world attack simulations against corporate networks.**

Learn **Advanced Persistent Threat (APT) tactics and adversary emulation.**

Offensive security mastery requires **continuous practice in real-world penetration testing environments and Capture The Flag (CTF) competitions.**

24.5 Defensive Cybersecurity Mastery: Blue Teaming and Threat Intelligence

Blue team cybersecurity professionals focus on **preventing, detecting, and responding to cyber attacks.**

24.5.1 Defensive Cybersecurity Specialization Path

Security Operations Center (SOC) Analyst Training

Learn **real-time security monitoring and log analysis**.

Tools: **Splunk, ELK Stack, IBM QRadar, Microsoft Sentinel**.

Incident Response and Threat Hunting

Investigate cyber incidents using **forensic analysis and SIEM threat intelligence**.

Tools: **Volatility, Autopsy, FTK Imager, MISP (Malware Information Sharing Platform)**.

Malware Analysis and Reverse Engineering

Analyze malware behavior using **sandboxing, static, and dynamic analysis techniques**.

Tools: **IDA Pro, Ghidra, Cuckoo Sandbox, PEStudio**.

Cloud Security and Zero-Trust Architecture

Secure **AWS, Azure, and Google Cloud environments**.

Implement **zero-trust security models for enterprise security**.

Defensive security mastery requires **real-world security monitoring experience and continuous training in advanced threat detection**.

24.6 Advanced Cybersecurity Specializations and Career Paths

24.6.1 High-Demand Cybersecurity Specializations

Specialization	Key Skills	Industry Demand
AI Security and Adversarial AI Defense	Securing AI models from cyber threats and AI-powered security automation	High
Quantum Cryptography and Post-Quantum Security	Implementing quantum-resistant encryption and cryptographic algorithms	Very High
Cyber Warfare and National Security Defense	Protecting military and government networks from nation-state cyber attacks	Very High
Blockchain and Smart Contract Security	Securing decentralized finance (DeFi), NFTs, and blockchain applications	High
Threat Intelligence and Cybercrime Analysis	Investigating global cybercriminal organizations and tracking dark web threats	High

Mastering cybersecurity requires **specialization in one or more advanced fields, depending on career goals and industry demand**.

24.7 The Path to Cybersecurity Leadership and Innovation

Cybersecurity mastery does not end with technical expertise. To **become an industry leader**, professionals must **develop strategic, leadership, and innovation-driven skills**.

24.7.1 Becoming a Cybersecurity Leader

1. **Develop Thought Leadership**

- Publish **cybersecurity research, threat reports, and industry whitepapers**.
- Engage in **public speaking, security conferences, and cybersecurity advisory roles**.

1. **Contribute to Open-Source Cybersecurity Projects**

- Collaborate with **global security communities to develop tools, frameworks, and research**.

1. **Pursue Executive-Level Cybersecurity Roles**

- Advance to roles such as **Chief Information Security Officer (CISO) or Cybersecurity Director**.

Cybersecurity leaders drive **innovation, policy-making, and large-scale security defense strategies** for governments and enterprises.

Conclusion

Cybersecurity mastery is **a continuous journey of learning, specialization, and real-world application**. Professionals must **develop foundational skills, master offensive and defensive security techniques, specialize in high-demand cybersecurity fields, and advance into leadership roles**.

The future of cybersecurity will be shaped by **AI-driven threat intelligence, quantum-resistant cryptography, cyber warfare defense, and blockchain security innovations**. Those who **adapt, innovate, and lead in cybersecurity will shape the future of global digital security**.

Chapter 25

HANDS-ON CYBERSECURITY LAB – SETUP AND PRACTICAL GUIDE

25.1 Introduction to the Hands-On Cybersecurity Lab

Mastering cybersecurity requires more than just theoretical knowledge. To become a skilled ethical hacker, penetration tester, or security expert, you need a dedicated lab environment to test tools, analyze vulnerabilities, and practice real-world attacks in a safe, controlled setting.

This chapter provides step-by-step instructions to configure a cybersecurity-focused laptop, install essential tools, set up virtual machines for testing, and automate security tasks using Python and Bash scripting.

By the end of this chapter, you will have a fully functional cybersecurity lab, allowing you to practice ethical hacking, penetration testing, digital forensics, and network security assessments safely.

25.2 Configuring a Laptop for Cybersecurity and Ethical Hacking

Before installing cybersecurity tools, ensure your laptop meets the recommended specifications for running penetration testing software, virtual machines, and security automation scripts.

25.2.1 Recommended Hardware and Software

25.2.2 Setting Up Kali Linux for Ethical Hacking

Kali Linux is the most widely used penetration testing OS, pre–installed with ethical hacking tools, security analyzers, and exploit frameworks.

Installing Kali Linux (Option 1: Direct Installation)

Download Kali Linux ISO from https://www.kali.org/downloads/.

Create a bootable USB using Rufus (Windows) or Etcher (Linux/Mac).

Boot into the USB and follow installation instructions.

Update the system after installation by running:

sudo apt update && sudo apt upgrade -y

Install essential security tools:

sudo apt install -y nmap wireshark metasploit-framework gobuster sqlmap john hydra

Setting Up Kali Linux in a Virtual Machine (Option 2: VM Installation)

Install VirtualBox or VMware on your system.

Download the Kali Linux VirtualBox image from https://www.kali.org/get-kali/#kali-virtual-machines.

Import the VM and allocate:

At least 4GB RAM

2 CPU cores

20GB storage space

Start Kali Linux and update the OS:

sudo apt update && sudo apt full-upgrade -y

25.3 Essential Cybersecurity Tools and Installations

25.3.1 Network Scanning and Reconnaissance

Nmap (Network Scanner)
  Nmap detects open ports, running services, and network vulnerabilities.
  Installation:

sudo apt install nmap -y

Usage:

nmap -sV -O 192.168.1.1

Wireshark (Network Packet Analyzer)
  Wireshark captures network traffic for deep packet inspection.
  Installation:

sudo apt install wireshark -y

Usage:
  sudo wireshark

25.3.2 Penetration Testing and Exploitation

Metasploit Framework (Exploitation Toolkit)
  Metasploit automates exploits, payload delivery, and vulnerability testing.
  Installation:

sudo apt install metasploit-framework -y

Start Metasploit:

msfconsole

John the Ripper (Password Cracking)
  John the Ripper cracks hashed passwords using brute force and dictionary attacks.
  Installation:

sudo apt install john -y

Usage:
  john —wordlist=/usr/share/wordlists/rockyou.txt hashfile.txt

25.4 Setting Up a Virtual Hacking Lab

To safely test security tools and hacking techniques, set up a virtual penetration testing lab.

25.4.1 Installing Virtual Machines for Hacking Practice

Install VirtualBox or VMware.

Download target systems:

Metasploitable 2
(https://sourceforge.net/projects/metasploitable/)

Damn Vulnerable Web App (DVWA) (http://www.dvwa.co.uk/)

Create an isolated network in VirtualBox:

Go to Network > Host-Only Adapter to prevent real-world network impact.

25.5 Running Cybersecurity Scripts for Automation

25.5.1 Python Script for Port Scanning

Save the following as **portscanner.py**:

Python:
```python
import socket
def scan_ports(target_ip):
print(f"Scanning {target_ip}...")
for port in range(1, 1025):
sock = socket.socket(socket.AF_INET, socket.SOCK_STREAM)
sock.settimeout(1)
result = sock.connect_ex((target_ip, port))
if result == 0:
print(f"Port {port} is open")
sock.close()
target = input("Enter target IP: ")
```

scan__ports(target)

Run the script:

python3 portscanner.py

25.6 Practicing Cybersecurity Techniques in Real-World Challenges

To refine your skills, practice with interactive cybersecurity platforms:

Hack The Box (https://www.hackthebox.com/)

TryHackMe (https://www.tryhackme.com/)

OverTheWire Wargames (http://overthewire.org/wargames/)

Conclusion

This chapter provides everything needed to set up a fully functional cybersecurity lab, install penetration testing tools, and automate security testing.
By following these steps, you will:

Configure your laptop for cybersecurity and ethical hacking.

Install and run essential security tools.

Practice penetration testing and network security assessments safely.

Automate security tasks using Python and Bash scripting.

This hands-on experience, combined with the strategic knowledge from previous chapters, will prepare you for real-world cybersecurity challenges and career opportunities.

Master cybersecurity. Apply what you learn. Stay ahead of cyber threats.

About the Author

As the founder of **The Alliance Society**, Elijah is committed to **developing cybersecurity training programs, ethical hacking courses, and cutting-edge cyber defense solutions**. His expertise spans **AI-powered cybersecurity automation, zero-trust security architectures, and advanced ethical hacking methodologies**.

With a passion for **digital security, ethical hacking, and cyber resilience**, Elijah's work provides **a roadmap for individuals and professionals to master cybersecurity, protect critical systems, and navigate the complexities of the digital world**.

You can connect with me on:
- https://thealliancesociety.org
- https://x.com/Elijah__L__Cooley
- https://facebook.com/ElijahLCooley

www.ingramcontent.com/pod-product-compliance
Lightning Source LLC
LaVergne TN
LVHW051232050326
832903LV00028B/2360